NOT AN ABLE-BODIED WHITE MAN WITH MONEY

*Expressions of Alternative Perspectives Influenced
by Experiences in Lehigh Valley, Pennsylvania*

edited by Angel R. Ackerman
with editorial assistance from Nancy Scott

Not an Able-Bodied White Man with Money: Expressions of
Alternative Perspectives Influenced by Experiences in Lehigh Valley, Pennsylvania
Copyright 2022 by Parisian Phoenix Publishing
ISBN: 978-1-7368782-5-5

Edited by Angel R. Ackerman, angel.ackerman@yahoo.com
Assistant Editor Nancy Scott

Cover Image: Heather Pasqualino Weirich; "All Of Me", 36" x 48", Oil on Canvas.

Published by Parisian Phoenix Publishing Company,
Easton, Pennsylvania USA
www.ParisianPhoenix.com

C O N N E C T with the publisher:
ParisianPhoenix
parisbirdbooks

In Memory of
Gommert James Ackerman, Sr.
whose quiet presence
and generous heart
impacted many.

September 30, 1948 – December 15, 2021

Contents

Aspiring for Community Between the Cleaved

By Angel R. Ackerman

The idea for this anthology came in the spring of 2021 as the world still recoiled from the shock of George Floyd's death and the rise of "Black Lives Matter" as a slogan instead of just a mission. It came about as the Covid-19 pandemic pretended to lessen in severity and left in its wake a need to "Stop Asian Hate" thanks to a president who referred to the illness as "the China virus." And then June rolled around, so we embrace the Pride of our LGBTQ+ brethren.

While I cannot deny the importance of these topics, the cleaving of society into special interest sub-groups disturbs me, because there are few of us that can say we do not belong to some minority group, especially in the United States, a land of large geographic range comprised of historical immigrants of one kind or another.

My own family, on my mother's side, hails from the British Isles. My mother's father came from England after World War II to marry my grandmother, and I have traced her family to Massachusetts in the early 1700s. This leads me to ascertain they are also probably English as my mother's family has no Native American blood that I have found. (Though according to my biological father's family via Facebook, he had some small portion of Native American heritage.)

According to that family legacy, I am primarily "White Anglo-Saxon Protestant" and my very own mother is first generation American. But judged only on what one sees in me, I easily belong to two groups that fight for equal rights—people assigned female at birth and people with disabilities.

(I have what is labeled as a mild case of hemiplegic Cerebral Palsy that interferes with my control of my lower body.) Other aspects of my identity may qualify for special attention: my socio-economic status (I was born into a blue collar family where our finances always teetered on the brink of poverty), my family's educational background (both my parents are high school drop-outs and college is not something many in my extended family have attended), addiction (while I am not an addict, both of my parents are alcoholics and smokers. Many in my extended family struggle with the abuse of alcohol and drugs.), and finally, religion (I have left my Protestant Christianity, after hanging out with the United Methodists, Moravians and Baptists, to profess my own beliefs in pagan animism).

So am I the majority? Or am I a member of minority groups? Or both? This book aims to explore various experiences in what we now call marginalized identities — a term that hadn't even entered the lexicon when the idea of this anthology was conceived. I had originally pitched the concept as a discussion of identity politics.

While Parisian Phoenix did eventually put out a call for pieces for this book, most of the submissions came from writers and artists recruited for their life experience. This anthology was first and foremost a collection of particular personal voices, not participants selected for their verbal or visual skills alone. This fulfills Parisian Phoenix's mission of representing and distributing "unique voices and diverse perspectives." Let that sink in for a minute. Parisian Phoenix seeks to say what no one else is saying, to say what no one else dares to say, to say what might not be popular or commercial.

In that same vein, after this essay you will find a list of bios for all of our contributors. These usually appear at the end of a nonfiction anthology or attached to each individual work. I have placed them in the front to orient the reader to who these people are. It might help the reader decide where they want to go in the text, but it also gives you a taste of who these people are beyond what you see in their carefully crafted contributions for this anthology.

At the end of the book, we have an index that will organize the pieces of the anthology by whether they are prose, poetry or art, but also coordinate the themes and list the authors. So, if you are looking for the voices regarding mental health or body image or disability, this will make it easy to find them.

This book seeks to remind us that there are very few people who have the inherent privilege that different groups tend to say others have. Dig deeper into any individual and you will find the thing that separates them from the whole. Hence the title of this book, *Not an Able-Bodied White Man with Money*. That seems to sum up who has the power and who doesn't.

The whole idea of community, like that of nation-states, is an invented concept. The more we splinter the identities that connect us, the less we have in common. And it takes a certain commonality to keep people together, in thought and practice. The more you carve people away from the whole, the harder it is to have a functioning society.

Difference exists. But difference cannot be labeled "good" or "bad," attaching values to difference sets a dangerous precedent because many of these differences cannot be changed. I cannot change my body. No amount of exercise or discipline will fix my body. It will, however, improve my health. That is a difference. But that same decree of difference may apply to someone fighting body image issues. Same exact statement. Completely different struggle.

What are the struggles in this volume? Let me tell you.

Blind essayist and poet Nancy Scott presents several prose pieces about disability, using her voice in "A Stab at Angels" to memorialize her brother and ask questions about long-term disability and short-term disability, how people adapt to their disabilities and also the intersection of family and disability.

She returns with mother-daughter pair, myself and Eva Parry, to offer three different views of an encounter at Dunkin Donuts five years ago in "The Nail Polish Story." While the piece is light and multi-faceted, it dabbles in our experiences with Nancy's blindness.

Her last piece is "Standing" where readers can attend with her a local veteran's day parade and feel the effect of time.

Author Seneca Blue contributes some art that explores body image.

Photographer Joan Zachary presents two photo series— one highlighting feminine forms and another capturing both my awkward gait and my relationship with my daughter, Eva Parry.

Art Director Gayle F. Hendricks offers a walk through the multi-ethnic blocks of her Southside Bethlehem neighborhood, complete with some insight from a Pennsylvania Dutch/Bethlehem Steel laborer's family's point of view.

Artist Nere Kapiteni shares her self portrait.

Screenwriter and novelist William Prystauk revisits exploring his own sexuality in a way that highlights commonality.

Poet Darrell Parry, father to Eva Parry, offers a poem that considers the impact his disability has had on his confidence.

Writer Tammy Burke explores a dark moment of fear from her youth and its effect on her mental health and growth.

Journalist Dawn Heinbach gives us several rich pieces, exploring her own journey with her weight and body image in "Devoured," while "Purging DNA" dips into the darkness of the violence within humanity, and in "Woke," she challenges those around her to see their privilege and end racism.

Author Rachel C. Thompson brings us on a journey through her mental health as she accepts her own identity as a queer woman and how this colors her experiences as she rebuilds her own life.

Jessica Dreistadt writes a poem about neurodivergence (the first piece she had written after earning her Ph.D.).

Thurston Gill, in his first official publication, offers two collections of short works that explore spirituality, philosophy, kindness and how to find/foster the best within oneself.

Mixed Media/Small Book Artist Maryann Riker allows us to reproduce her women's suffrage postcards.

Maryann Ignatz chronicles her family history through three generations at Steve's Cafe, from her own Hungarian heritage to twentieth century life in working class Phillipsburg, a transportation center for the trains and Morris Canal.

I myself write about this country's tendency to judge people on their work and how much money they have.

My daughter, Eva Parry, explores disability shaming and disability acceptance even as she faces the fact that she will soon have hearing aids.

And then there is Jan Krieger. Jan has a theme I'm sure many people can understand— she's tired of being the "yes man." She brings some much needed humor to these serious themes.

Tiffani Velez brings us with her on a medical journey through years of misdiagnosis which she attributes to her invisibility resulting from her femaleness.

And our cover, that lovely abstract swirl of shapes that coincide and narrow within, a combination of curves and angles, hard and soft. That comes to us from artist Heather Pasqualino Weirich. Heather has and parents a child with ADHD.

Everyone in this volume honors Parisian Phoenix with their offering, and I hope this project is one of many that can explore topics and generate conversations.

As humans, we need to embrace the complexity of our multi-facetedness. I may identify as CIS-gendered female, "straight," a parent, a spouse and probably eventually a divorcee, disabled, underemployed, overeducated, American of British descent, an academic and a member of Generation X, but not a single one of those labels defines me as a person. Instead, they create a kaleidoscopic plumage that make me who I am and allow me to empathize with a broad number of other people.

Marginalized identities must be a strength, because even if we never intend to do it, we all become advocates, always for ourselves and often for others.

Contributors

ANGEL ACKERMAN had a 15-year career in print journalism and has dabbled in creative and travel writing throughout her life. She has a B.A. in English language and literature (and French) from Moravian College, a B.A. in international affairs from Lafayette College, and has taken graduate level courses in world history at West Chester University, specializing in post-colonial Francophone Africa and Muslim relations.

Angel's nonprofit involvement includes fostering cats with Feline Urban Rescue and Rehab, communications oversight at anti-human-trafficking group ASPIRE to Autonomy, and past volunteering on the board of Mary Meuser Memorial Library and Greater Lehigh Valley Writers Group (GLVWG). Her professional nonprofit career includes public relations and "tech" curriculum development at the YWCA of Bethlehem, communications and fundraising work at anti-poverty, literacy entity ProJeCt of Easton, and community relations and alumni publications at Lafayette College.

Her previous publications at Parisian Phoenix include *Manipulations* and *Courting Apparitions,* volume 1 & 2 of the Fashion and Fiends series. *Recovery,* volume 3 of the series, is scheduled to release on Valentine's Day.

She has been featured in *Dime Store Review*'s 10-word stories, *StepAway Magazine, Rum Punch Press, Global Studies South, Hippocampus Magazine,* The Mighty, Yahoo News and the *SAGE Encyclopedia of Poverty.*

TAMMY BURKE, a former officer of the Greater Lehigh Valley Writers Group (GLVWG), has served as both president and as chair for a record sold-out "Write Stuff" conference and pre-con workshops. She has published over 400 articles and has interviewed celebrities, agents, editors, authors and others. In addition to having served as Critique Coordinator for the Society of Book Writers and Illustrators (SCBWI) for the Lycoming County chapter, she runs various writer brainstorming groups and is currently a member of Apex, a science fiction and fantasy mentoring association that was run by *New York Times* bestselling author, David Farland before his unexpected death in January 2022.

Tammy is currently finishing her YA Epic Fantasy manuscript *Faeries Don't Lie.* She can also be found with a sword in her hand in medieval-style fencing tournaments and melees. See photos after her essay.

SENECA BLUE is the pseudonym of an anonymous writing duo with roots in the Lehigh Valley. Seneca wrote Parisian Phoenix's first contemporary romance, *Trapped.* One half of the pair has lost and gained more than 100 pounds during her lifetime. Both are clumsy and appreciate nature.

6

JESSICA R. DREISTADT, Ph.D. is based in Easton, Pa. She is the founding director of The Fruition Coalition and the author of 11 books about leadership and social change. Her recently completed dissertation, *Portraits of Women Leaders: Solidarity and Social Division in Progressive Social Movement Organizations*, explored the complex ways that identities both constrain and facilitate relationships. To connect with Jessica, visit jessicardreistadt.com.

THURSTON D. GILL JR. went from law enforcement to various aspects of the security industry: healthcare &

campus security, loss prevention, a private security contractor, and security training & development management. Thurston was ordained as a minister more than 30 years ago and invested several years of life as a mental health recovery specialist and an intensive case manager. He says he has been blessed with opportunities that enabled him to acquire experiences and skills that he enjoys sharing at every opportunity through workshops, groups, and other training activities.

DAWN HEINBACH's writing focuses on social issues and the people affected by them. Her nonfiction tends to highlight regular people who are improving their communities or making a positive change in some way. Dawn's interests are influenced by her life experiences; she grew up and spent most of her adult life in

a small rural town that sorely lacked in diversity. Before returning to college as a (very) nontraditional student, Dawn worked in a textile dye house, a copper wire factory, and a steel bar factory. She also owned and operated a coffee shop.

Dawn holds an M.A. in Publishing from Rosemont College and is currently completing a second M.A. in journalism at New York University.

In 2016, her poem "Stunning" earned an award from the English department at her undergraduate alma mater, Kutztown University of Pennsylvania.

In 2015, Dawn founded Writing Wrongs, a 501(c)(3) nonprofit that facilitates a literary journalism program for college students. She lives in Berks County with her partner of 25 years and their two rescue cats.

GAYLE F. HENDRICKS discovered her love

of art via a 64-box of Crayola crayons and a Spirograph. She thought she'd be an architect or an art teacher when she grew up but an non-traditional educational trajectory—A.A. from Northampton Community College, B.A. in sociology from Cedar Crest College, M.F.A. from Marywood University—led to a career in graphic design.

She began her career setting signs in a local department store (and fell in love with typography), moved into advertising, and eventually got a job at a local print shop in the paper era. Production in that print shop introduced her to a machine called the Mac IIci and Gayle learned very early the art of computerized graphic design and publishing.

When she's not working with authors or doing volunteer work for nonprofits, she teaches graphic design at local community colleges and universities.

MARYANN STEPHANIE IGNATZ was born on her mother's birthday, November 3, in 1946. The only child of Steve and Mary (Sipos) Ignatz, Maryann graduated Phillipsburg High School and Moravian College. She taught Spanish and English in the Easton Area School District for almost a decade before he father's death in February 1977.

Since then, she has been the proprietor of Steve's Cafe, a shot and beer, working man's bar at 766 South Main Street in Phillipsburg, N.J. The business has been in her family for more than 100 years.

She has a special interest in preserving history, especially that of the railroad and the Morris Canal. She also plays a mean game of quoits.

NERE KAPITENI is an animator / motion graphics artist and illustrator originally from Tanzania in East Africa. In childhood, a pencil, sketchbook and escaping into nature were all she needed to disappear into a world of her making, keeping her entertained for hours.

She received her B.A. of Fine Arts and B.S. in Environmental Science at University of Massachusetts-Amherst and M.A. in Computer Animation at New York Institute of Technology in New York City.

Though she had set a path in environmental studies, she couldn't go without art in her life for long. Therefore, she pursued a career in the arts with a concentration in animation. Illustration had been her main form of expression, and now had a way to bring her drawings to life!

Her ultimate goal is to use her illustration and animation to create educational media promoting positive social change and environmental awareness.

She lives in Easton, Pa., with her husband and black cat, Oya.

8

JAN KRIEGER is *not* a best selling novelist. After a 30-plus-year career in the travel industry, she is now happily learning the craft of being a chocolatier (and sampling all of that deliciousness). She graduated from Wilson Area High School, holds a B.A. in Russian from Lafayette College, an M.A. in Slavic Languages and Literatures from Pennsylvania State University, and a certificate of travel and tourism from Northampton Community College— in that order.

An active volunteer, Jan serves as vice president of the Wilson Area school board of directors, as a trustee at NCC, and a member of the Wilson Area Partners in Education Foundation. In her spare time, she loves to travel, workout, read, and spoil her Morkie, the one and only (her ladyship), Sobaka.

EVA PARRY is a high school senior hoping to enter the dog training business. She fosters cats for Feline Urban Rescue and Rehab and works for Apricity Pet Care. A low brass musician, she spent four years in marching band and seven years in concert band. After graduation, she hopes to pursue a course in auto mechanics or other trade before attending Lafayette College to study psychology or Moravian University for education.

DARRELL PARRY is a writer, artist and event organizer. He founded the online publication *Stick Figure Poetry Quarterly* and the monthly Stick Figure Poetry open mic. He also co-hosts Lehigh Valley Poetry's Virtual Salon, which currently meets on Zoom the first Monday of every month. His alter ego works in higher education, not as a professor, but as one of those reviled peddlers of unaffordable course materials. Believe it or not, he even sometimes sells poetry books.

His first full-length poetry manuscript, *Twists: Gathered Ephemera*, is available through Parisian Phoenix Publishing.

WILLIAM D. PRYSTAUK is the award-winning author of the Kink Noir crime thriller series and has received international acclaim for his screenplays. He is also co-host of the long-running *The Last Knock* horror podcast and his articles on the horror movies have appeared in scholarly journals. Currently, he is in pre-production of his first feature film. Originally from northern New Jersey, Bill now resides in northeast Pennsylvania where he works as a full-time medical copy-writer.

When not writing, he enjoys photography and sushi, and con-siders dark chocolate a major food group of its own. The Kink Noir series—*Bloodletting, Punishment, Debauchery* and *Bondage*—is avail-able on Amazon.com.

MARYANN RIKER is a mixed-media artist whose collages and artist books contrast historical images and ephemera with mod-ern social issues. Her works are in many public and private collections and exhibits her work throughout the Lehigh Valley and New York area. She is currently honing her skills in miniature watercolor, wearing out many paint brushes and working on becom-

ing a legend in her own living room.

NANCY SCOTT is an essayist and poet. Her more than 925 bylines have appeared in magazines, literary journals, anthologies and newspapers includ-ing: *AIM Magazine, The Aurorean, Black Fox Literary Magazine, Blue Unicorn, Breath and Shadow, Braille Forum, Braille Monitor, Burnside Review, ByLine, Chrysan-themum, Church Educator, Contemporary Haibun Online, Cup of Comfort for Inspiration, Cup of Comfort for Women, Dialogue Magazine, Disabilities Studies Quarterly, Disability Rag, The Express-Times, Kaleidoscope, The Lion, The Lutheran Journal, Magnets and Ladders,* The Mighty (which publishes regularly to Yahoo News), Nature-Writing.com, *Newsreel, One Sentence Poems, Opening Stages, Palo Alto Review, The Philadelphia Inquirer, Philadelphia Stories, The Ragged Edge,*

Sacred Journey, Stone Voices, Shark Reef, The Sun, Thema, Whistling Fire, and *Wordgathering.* Nan has also published numerous audio commentaries including essays for public radio station WDIY.

She received First Prize in the 2009 Inter-national Onkyo Braille Essay Contest. Her poetry chapbook *Hearing the Sunrise* (Anderie Press, 1996) was exhibited in 1997 by The Very Special Arts Gallery in Wash-ington, D.C. Two of the poems from *Hearing the Sunrise* appear in the disability anthology *Staring Back* (Plume, 1997). Her second chapbook, *Leveling the Spin,* was published in 2006, and she has collaborated with artist Maryann Riker to create several chapbooks including *The Nature of Beyond* (2010) and *The Almost Abecedarian* (2015).

Nan regularly performs readings before live audiences. When not writing, she is an avid follower of NASA and would like to have been an astro-naut or a journalist in NASA's Public Affairs office in another life.

RACHEL C. THOMPSON

is an outdoorswoman, avid reader/researcher, former long-distance runner, former street clown and theme park performer, construction owner, project manager, exotic dancer, fishermen, expert canoeist, cold weather camper, Air Force veteran, single parent, short order cook, sunset fanatic, hunter/trapper, recreation vehicle (RV) dweller, motorcyclist, formally wealthy, poor often, and a nerd.

Mental breakdowns and a motorcycle crash forced Rachel out of industry but art doesn't care about that. The stuff Rachel always did anyway for fun is what she does now, or more accurately, it's what she is. Writer, painter, musician, they all fit. Building was fun, too.

Rachel has four novels and one anthology in print and e-book. She lives the old hippie arts-and-crafts low budget life well off the beaten path—the starving artist.

To learn more about her books, visit rcthom.com. But be forewarned — she hasn't learned the art of webpages.

TIFFANI BURNETT VELEZ's

first novel, *Budapest*, was featured at Annual Conference of Jewish Librarians, her novella *A Berlin Story*, held Amazon Bestseller rank in Historical Fiction for three months, and her novel *All This Time* was voted Best Goodreads Military Fiction Read in 2015.

She is a Professor of English and ESL at Lehigh Carbon Community College and is the Program Director of English Language Foundations at Berks Technical Institute. Her short fiction has appeared in *Toe Good Poetry, The Feminine Collective,* and *Nicean Magazine*. She was a freelance writer for more than 20 years and her work has appeared in *Country Discoveries, Pennsylvania Magazine,* Yahoo! News, *Conde' Nast Portfolio,* and many more online and print magazines and newspapers in North America, Europe, and Africa.

HEATHER PASQUALINO WEIRICH

is a fine art painter creating works ranging from Abstract Expressionism to Contemporary Impressionism.

Her landscape paintings are inspired by the ever-changing colors and light of the Pacific Northwest in addition to the rich rolling topography of her childhood home of Pennsylvania.

Heather's abstract works can best be described as: a physical manifestation of an ongoing personal journey to sustain a healthy emotional state of wellbeing through the use of color, movement & art.

Heather has lived in various parts of eastern Pennsylvania and the Pacific Northwest. Currently, she resides in Valley Forge, Pa., with her husband, two children and a menagerie of domestic pets and wild creatures.

While she is not creating, she works at a nonprofit in Phoenixville, Pa., and competes in Enduro and Cross-Country Mountain Bike races.

She is a co- founder and co-head coach for a local youth mountain bike team and is president of More Kids on Bikes 501(c)(3) a nonprofit entity dedicated to getting more kids on bikes and keeping them there!

JOAN ZACHARY was born in upstate New York and moved to Pennsylvania in 1974. She has been intrigued by photography since childhood, but she is also a musician and writer. Currently Joan lives in Point Phillips, Pennsylvania with her fiancé, musician Randall Smith, one very photogenic cat, and the many residents of Plastiqueville.

A Stab At Angels

By Nancy Scott

For Mark Mullowney, 1956–2003

I play your Sinatra CDs, wandering among your wanton drugs and love and God and knees that work and effortless thinness and chore-less money and no more heart cath. I know you by the ladybug magnets on my fridge—you who hated chotchkies but couldn't resist sneaking lucky critters into my new apartment.

I still get dressed soon after waking up because of your 8 a.m. calls. I'd say, "I'm up; I'm up."

"But are you dressed yet?" was your too-knowing come back. You, I suspect in this time you called "retirement," were never dressed in the morning. You never held a long-term job, preferring bartender, driver, sleazy phone fundraiser, and other types of nomadic employment. But for me, you were more teacher than doer.

No one else easily answers my mundane questions that only a blind person has. "Look at QVC." "What color is stone? And is there anything really neutral?" "Where's the stock market?" "What is the name of that restaurant we like on Sixth Street?"

No one else will drive to fast food for my first-day-of-summer whim or to find ice cream. No one else would drive me to poetry readings in a snow storm (of course, you bitched about it the whole time and then, years later, didn't remember doing it.)

In the end, which of us was more disabled? I was born blind and you were always heavy. You tried to teach me to build Lincoln Log mansions. You let me play with Matchbox cars and trucks. But you wouldn't take me along once you could freely cross streets. When you were little, you were afraid of the dark.

Did I become your excuse for bad behaviors? Did you live too fast and like close edges? Eventually, you became diabetic and unable to walk much. Maybe you became too used to painkillers.

Maybe your love of cooking, but not love of vegetables, didn't help.

No one else knows what a younger brother knew. You always said you didn't want to be the "last man standing." I didn't understand then, but as last person in our family, I understand now.

Will I someday be where you are, looking down and helping the living I care about? I hear you waving at me in sneaky wind chime rifts, pinging one or two notes so softly that I must be still to know you move the orphaned air. And you put my hands on things I've lost.

Have you forgiven the Universe for making you the able-bodied sibling?

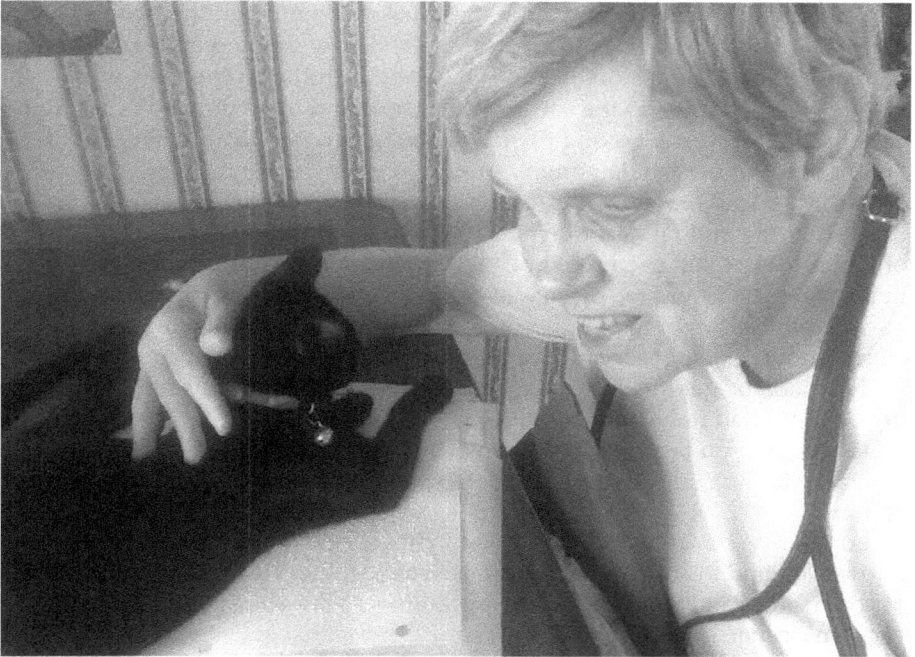

The author cuddles foster kitten Shady. Nan says Shady "gets it" about blindness. Shady, rescued and socialized by volunteers of Feline Urban Rescue and Rehab, joined her FURRever family in November 2021.

My blindness got me more attention and a free pass to college. More importantly, it forced my discipline.

Do you have hands and knees? Does any part of you ache or clog now? What do you wait for?

Will I see in the Astral? Or will I still be the listener injecting my life to mostly strangers on paper? Speaking of paper, when I showed you my first book, you said, "Well, I won't have to sue you over anything." And you said once that, if I died first, the first thing you'd do is find someone to read my Braille journals. Those notebooks still reside on the top shelf of the book cabinet you picked out and built. And yes, the cabinet top is wrong side out. Do you have paper?

Have you talked to our parents? Do they get along better in the Astral? Was I the milkman's child? Why did the men die so early?

I've always wanted to tell this story: We were in the grocery store. You used the store's scooter; I walked behind you holding the back handles with my white cane visible. "Blind-O and the Fatman," you'd say. We wanted that sale-priced TV dinner that your six-foot-five self couldn't reach sitting. You directed me "left, one more left, now up." I got right to the shelf, but I couldn't quite reach. I started to laugh. You chuckled until another male shopper came along and told us we were having too much fun and easily reached up for the boxes. I had laughed myself to tears, but you were now unhappy. This surprised me. It was, I think, the difference between a long-term disability and having to adjust to one later in life. You felt the absence of your ability more.

Your only writing compliment to me was "oh I'd much rather feed a houseful of people than write an article." And why did you and our parents hate broccoli? (Thanks goodness my husband introduced me to healthy veggies.) And there was the coconut cream pie and the crumbled crust. You couldn't take a weird looking pie for other sighted people! You were mad and I got to eat the whole yummy thing.

Our last actual time together, almost a week before you died, was a beautiful May Sunday morning at Parkway Diner. We split an order of pancakes but still used too much butter and syrup. You brought the newspaper flyers and we discussed coupons and shopping strategies. You narrated the antics of the toddler in the booth behind us who kept eating sugar from the dispenser and popping up on his knees to smile and babble at us. He made us glad we had no children. We both had visions of his difficult future. But I had no visions of mine.

How could you be gone at 46? How could you survive heart surgery, stomach stapling, and two car accidents only to have your heart stop quietly at home?

Terry took your cat litter, your TV, your almost new microwave, the good throw rugs, and the big freezer which used to be mine. Vicky took two car loads of your clothes and sealed meds to New Bethany Ministries. Pam loved your vacuum cleaner. I brought home the carousel horse that matches mine, your paper shredder, lots of food (15 cans of tuna fish) and paper products. Your death left a different hole than losing husband and parents. No spontaneity. No wacky wisdom. Sue said, "Mark would want you to be happy." Would you? You would want me to not be stupid and to be braver. And productive?

My pages turned to seasons. Now, I have outlived all of you. I am older than our mother was. Sixty-three and beyond feels momentous but I can't tell if it's in a good way.

What is courage? What is inertia? What is perseverance? What is legacy? I didn't smoke or drink much. I got all the family hair. I saved money and had the same phone number for more than 30 years. (Your passwords were always parts of my phone number.) My life here looks small, but, I hope, valuable.

I can't imagine being helpful in the Astral. Is that why I'm not there?

▶ Nancy Scott's more than 925 essays and poems have appeared in magazines, literary journals, anthologies, newspapers, and as audio commentaries. Her latest chapbook appears on Amazon, *The Almost Abecedarian*. She won First Prize in the 2009 International Onkyo Braille Essay Contest. Recent work appears in *Black Fox Literary Magazine*, *Braille Forum*, *Chrysanthemum*, *Kaleidoscope*, *One Sentence Poems*, *Shark Reef*, *Wordgathering*, and Yahoo News.

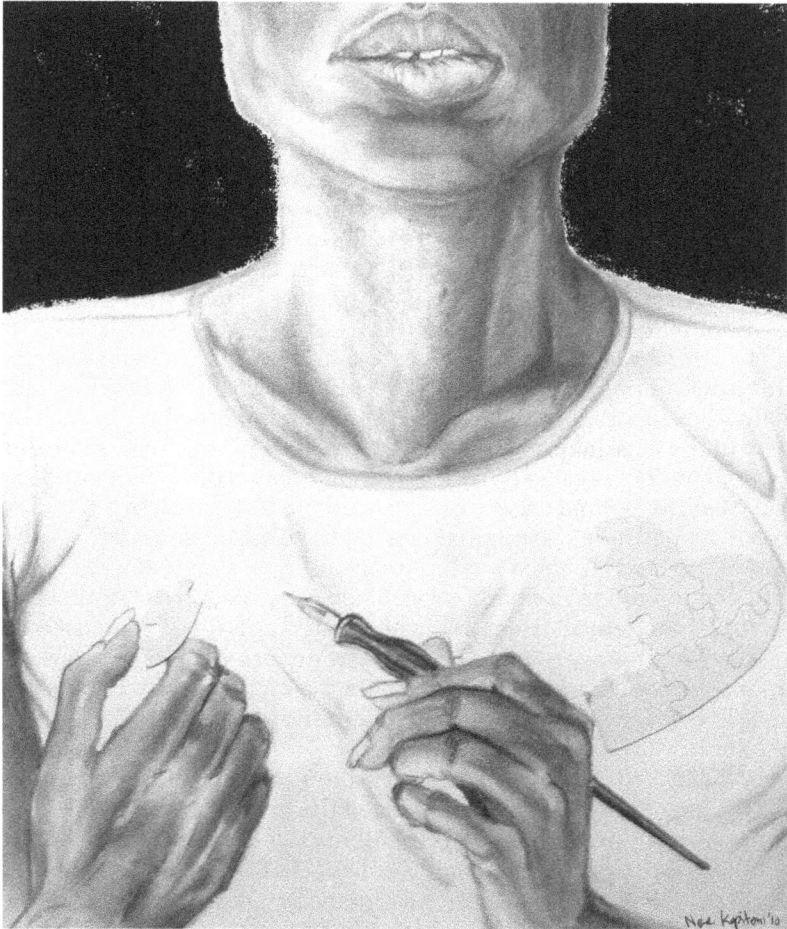

Nere Kapiteni, *Puzzled Pieces,* 2010

▶ Nere Kapiteni is an animator/motion graphics artist and illustrator originally from Tanzania in East Africa. She received her B.A. of Fine Arts and B.S. in Environmental Science at University of Massachusetts-Amherst and M.A. in Computer Animation at New York Institute of Technology in New York City. Her ultimate goal is to use her illustration and animation to create educational media promoting positive social change and environmental awareness.

Commonality

by William D. Prystauk

Growing up in northern New Jersey, right outside of New York City, blessed me in many ways.

In the 1980s, Kearny was a small Scot-Irish town, but my classmates included a large Latin population and Indians as well. But in my junior and senior years of high school, I often visited New York's Greenwich Village via the Path train out of nearby Harrison. The short ride allowed me to explore punk and alternative shops, and I fell completely in love with the ultra-diverse population flowing in and out of Washington Square Park.

But as a young man, I wanted to know who I was. Once I had that definitive definition, I would know where I belonged. This longing had originally developed out of fear. I had long hair and loved punk rock but very few of my classmates had become immersed in the music genre, and a daily regimen of Advanced Dungeon and Dragons placed me into a nerd category that my honors classes only exacerbated. Regardless, I felt "lost."

Internally, I had some issues that needed to be addressed. With that long hair and a lithe body, I had a feminine sensibility, which made me question both my gender and my sexuality. I also had other concerns because I had desires for bondage and discipline, which had come about at an early age. All of this added up to me trying to understand my orientation. However, there was no internet at the time and I did not know of any resources that could help me. There was no way for me to determine what any of these feelings meant — and if I was "normal" or not.

I never had "the talk" with my parents about sex, and relied on a book called "Teenage Sexuality" that showcased the fundamentals about body parts and disease and pregnancy, but not much more. It wasn't until I got a hold of Dr. Alex Comfort's "The Joy of Sex" that I found some relief. As soon as I came to an illustration of a woman bound to a bed, I learned that bondage was a "normal" thing for some people.

The sudden relief had brought me to tears. The feelings I had endured since early childhood about bondage and discipline were "okay." There were others out there with the same orientation. I was no longer alone.

Even so, my fluid sexuality affected my thinking in major ways thanks to rabid homophobia from seemingly every adult, and from men in cloth screeching from pulpits. I felt damned and became depressed.

But Greenwich Village saved me. On my many trips to the city, I saw gay couples living their lives. Heading into the "gay section" around Christopher Street allowed me to witness a vibrant counter-culture where homosexuality was the norm.

I was still afraid, for both my soul and how others would perceive me. I had a couple of gay classmates, as well as a few gay teachers, and it never resonated with me that these people had been accepted and weren't targeted by others, from classmates to parents. I had not seen or heard any overt prejudice. Yet, I still thought it best not to ask questions or seek any sort of guidance. Fear had overwhelmed me.

As a young writer, I took the Path on my own to Washington Square one day because I wanted to sit and listen to people. I had to eavesdrop and hear their own words. That warm day in the summer, I traipsed through the park and listened to a lesbian couple, the Rastafarians tossing a Frisbee around, gay men on the move — a Leatherdaddy offered me drugs and a gay businessman ogled me. I followed a transvestite for a while, and bowed out of respect to a Voodoo priestess and her entourage.

Everyone I came across that day spoke of the same things: finances, employment, grocery shopping, fashion, and love. The same things anyone would talk about during the course of the day.

This is when I realized we're all the same. All normal. All carbon-based oxygen breathing lifeforms that make up the human race. Color didn't matter, neither did gender, ethnicity, class, religious belief, political affiliation, sexual orientation, or any other category that could be used as a divisive weapon.

Any prejudices I had died that day.

And that entire "human race is one" became confirmed years later when I witnessed a car accident on a corner in Washington Heights. Primarily a Dominican community in the early 90s, Dominicans and East Europeans ran to the cars to make certain the occupants were fine. The Asian couple was okay and so were people in the other car. A rabbi on the corner looked to the sky, held out his hands and proclaimed, "Thank God nobody was hurt!"

People are people.

Even so, it took me many moons to cast aside all those labels to all of those "tribes" I felt the need to belong to: punk rocker, man, American, left-of-the-dial political enthusiast, Italian/Ukrainian, atheist, and a sexually-oriented devotee of a kink lifestyle.

The idea of political correctness helped me expunge all labels. That happened when I understood that placing people into particular categories means that the bullet points defining each pigeonhole may compel people to adopt particular ways of thinking. I may enjoy bondage, but I don't want to be bound by someone else's definitions.

Today, I wave no flags or banners, embrace no categories or manifestos, and I do not support any groups, organizations, or political leaders.

I am just a person and support everyone in their individual quest to live their best life — as long as they are of great character and bring no harm to others.

This is why the "diversity and inclusion" ideal, although a very good one, missed a step on the ladder. We must celebrate our commonality first and foremost. Once we realize we all bleed the same and need the same things to survive: food, clothing, shelter, and love, we can better see, accept, and appreciate all of those unique things that make us different and special.

Only then may bigotry in all its ugly forms may fall by the wayside forever.

And a rebirth of social discourse devoid of hate and hostility can bring us together like we never imagined.

▶ William D. Prystauk is an award-winning author of the Kink Noir crime thriller series and has received international acclaim for his screenplays. Originally from northern New Jersey, Prystauk now resides in northeast Pennsylvania where he works as a full-time medical copywriter.

Small and Crooked

By Darrell Parry

Everybody has something…
some issue with their appearance:

the need to lose weight,
a nose that's too large,
an unsightly mole or scar that mars
otherwise flawless skin.

The reality is, that these are details most people
will take note of and decide to ignore,
but that niggling fear of judgment always persists.

The pervasive thought that someone
might linger upon our imperfections,
even if we are not outwardly mocked or ridiculed for them,
is something that we internalize,
often without realizing it.

There came a time when I had to admit it.

Yes, most of my shyness,
my introverted tendencies,
my insecurities, and lack of confidence
probably stem in some way from my physical handicap.

It's not something that had ever occurred to me
because my short, crooked arm
is not a thing that I think about.

The disfigurement is just there.
It's always been there.
I have incorporated it into my identity
like a tattoo with great personal significance.

It has does not limit me—
I lugged around 50 lb. boxes for a living—
so its value, or lack thereof,
is mostly peripheral.

My weird arm is part of who I am
and I would not change it
even if I could.

But it's there and it's visible
and it's obvious.
and if it's like a tattoo, then it is one
that I'm not sure everyone will appreciate
the way that I do.

That is where the insecurities come in.

I wear long sleeves
and I prefer meeting people
over texts and Zooms
and I don't like pictures of myself.

Because like most people with their flaws
I try to hide it,
cover it up when I meet people,
like body jewelry at a job interview.

So, maybe I tend to avoid
talking to people I don't know
and maybe I stick quietly
to the back of crowded rooms
and maybe I say "no,"
when my daughter wants to paint my nails black
for Halloween.

I tell her that my hands are not something
I am inclined to draw attention to
and she says,
"Oh, right,"
because she didn't consider that.

Because
it's not a thing that she thinks about.
It's just a hand to her
and, small and crooked as it is,
it's part of her father's identity.

And she remembers
how when she was a child
she would hold hands with him
and that hand was little like hers
and it would fit just right.

She loved it because of that
and she loves it still for giving her that memory.

That very fact should teach me something,

Should tell me that
perhaps that flawed part of me
might fit just right
in other people's lives as well
or at worst,
might simply be taken note of
and ignored, rendered inconsequential
in the wake of familiarity.

It should inspire me to meet new people
every chance I get
and to call attention to myself
in crowded rooms
and to say "yes,"
when my daughter wants to paint my nails black
for Halloween.

Because the people who love us also love our flaws
for being a part of us.

Maybe the most important lesson of all
that I need to learn is that only thing
truly small and crooked about me,
is my perception of myself.

▶ Darrell Parry is a writer, artist and event organizer. He founded the online publication Stick Figure Poetry Quarterly and the monthly Stick Figure Poetry open mic. He holds a B.A. in English from Moravian College,. and works at Lafayette College. His first full-length poetry manuscript, Twists: Gathered Ephemera, is available through Parisian Phoenix.

When A Tree Twists

By Tammy Burke

Fear came to me when I was six-years-old as a twisted tree, warped and ancient. It lived a half mile away from my house, beyond the railroad tracks along an old dirt path. I could never bear to go passed it alone, especially after nightfall. Its limbs hung like murderous hands, stretching out to hurt, to maim, to kill. And it had a face. No other trees had a face. But it was its overwhelming presence that frightened me most. I could feel it looking through me to my very heart and I trembled at the pleasure it took.

It watched me. It didn't stay locked into place like any other tree. It warped itself. It tiptoed on gnarly tree roots down the path to my house. Yes, I was afraid of the shadowy figure who crept and lingered in my closet, staying quiet except for the occasional creak, motionless, except for the occasional thump, until all the grownups went away and the lights went out. But when the lights went out, I didn't know whether it would be the dark killer or if it would be the tree. The shadow killer would jump out of my closet to shoot me. I could lock my closet door or at least, I remember a lock. The tree though, it would push itself twisting through all the knotholes in my paneling with skinny knobby arms and jabby long fingered hands and it would rend me apart. There was no way to lock it out. I never slept near any of the walls.

Perhaps its coincidental that the fear of that tree happened around the same time as when my uncle was murdered. Over a five-dollar pool bet. Shot five times. Stood over by his killer until he bled out. His wife's jaw blown off. Their baby temporarily missing. My aunt, oozy bandages cradled about her crippled face, found sleeping a top my uncle's grave while my very pregnant mother cared for her dead brother's screaming baby son. And the drinking establishment where my uncle died, changing its name to 'Last Chance Saloon.' The grisly details are lengthy even when recited in short sentences and as many times as I heard my mother crying into the phone as her grief spilled out, I knew them. I knew every sentence. I knew them all.

And more sentences came until my mother blended into the dark story and functioned without really being there. Six is so early to try to figure out how to fill in the gaps. How to keep a family together. I had no power. I couldn't make my mother smile but I could keep from causing her more harm. I kept my feelings to myself. I didn't talk about my fears. I didn't talk about my sorrow. I slept on the edge of my bed away from my wall, closet door firmly shut and locked. And eventually I turned into a tower-Rapunzel with thick border walls until that tree stopped returning to its daytime spot to mock me during waking hours.

Perhaps the tree was cut down. Perhaps it was burned. Whatever the reason, the empty place to this day still creaks and I can see its quivering twisted arms in my mind's eye. But it is not fear that I face. I do not know what it is but it is not fear.

▶ Tammy Burke, fantasy author, has worked within the Greater Lehigh Valley Writers Group (GLVWG), the Society of Book Writers and Illustrators (SCBWI) Lycoming County chapter, and Apex, a science fiction and fantasy mentoring association.. Tammy is currently finishing her YA Epic Fantasy manuscript *Faeries Don't Lie*. She can also sometimes be found with a sword in her hand in medieval-style fencing tournaments and melees.

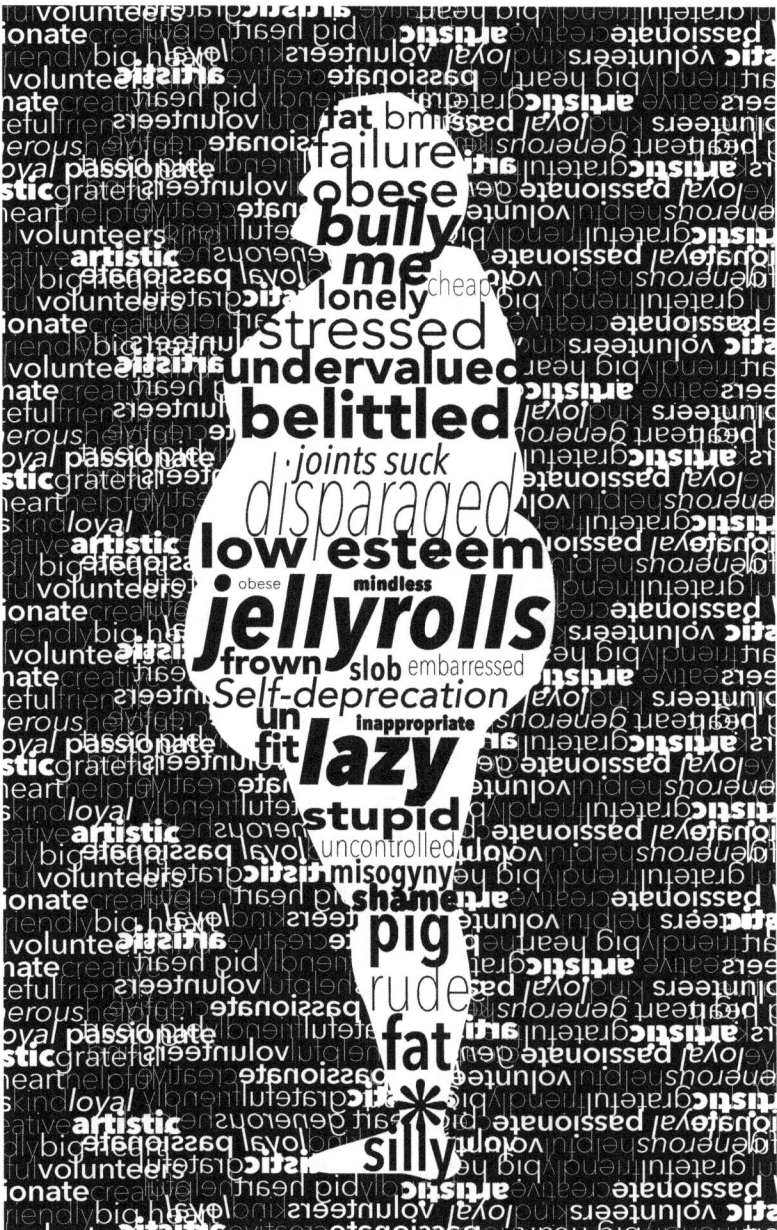

Seneca Blue, *Inside/Outside*, 2021

> ▶ Seneca Blue is the pseudonym of an anonymous writing duo with roots in the Lehigh Valley. Seneca wrote Parisian Phoenix's first contemporary romance, *Trapped*. One half of the pair has lost and gained more than 100 pounds several times during her lifetime. Both are clumsy and appreciate nature and art..

Devoured

By Dawn Heinbach

When I was eight
I liked to go outside at night
after it rained
and shine a flashlight on the ground.
I would see earthworms slip back into the earth
when the beam hit them.
They were fat.
We would catch some, the neighbor boys and I,
to use when we went fishing.
My dad told me that the large rectangle
on the worms' bodies was the heart.
Their heart chambers encircled a portion of their pink, plump bodies,
even fatter than they were.

In fourth grade, I was sent on an errand by the teacher
during class.

                            and library were.
                   where the cafeteria
            to the fourth floor,
      all the stairs
I walked up

Since there were no other students in the halls,
I thought it didn't matter
which   side
I walked on.
An older boy approached on my side, going the opposite direction.
I smiled at him.
People said I was too shy.
I thought I would try being friendly.
"Get on your own side, ya big lug!" he growled.
I learned my lesson about looking people in the eye,
trying to be friendly.

In the department store dressing room, my mother struggled
to close the button on the pants I was trying on.
I loathed shopping. I didn't care about clothes.
"You've got to lose weight.

You will have to go to the next size."
This scene played out every year before school started.
I heard my mother telling her sister
on the phone that she had to buy Huskie pants for me.

There was a heavy girl in my class.
(Every class has one.)
In fifth grade,
kids started calling her

whale.

This was her name until we graduated high school.
I don't know if people still call her that.
I believed I was fat,
but I could feel better about myself because
at least I wasn't as fat as the **whale**.

My birthday was in the summer.
When I was ten, one of my birthday gifts was
a heart-shaped cork bulletin board that I could paint.
(I was very good at art.)
I painted the board and my mom hung it in the kitchen
above the table.
Love, it said in curly red letters.
One night at supper the conversation turned
to my weight.
"I'll give you ten dollars if you lose ten pounds,"
My dad said.
He took a ten-dollar bill from his wallet
and pinned it to the board.
"You have one month to lose the weight."
Thirty days went by, and I still weighed the same.
My dad took the bill down.
I failed to earn the ten dollars.
I failed to lose ten pounds.
Why hadn't I tried harder?

The ad in the teen magazine was **bold**: colorful embroidery
on the back pocket of a denim jean,
worn by a girl who was definitely not fat.
Fight fat, the embroidery said in
pink, blue, green, red, and yellow.
It was pretty.

The way you lost weight in those days was to stop eating.
You counted calories and didn't eat foods that were bad.
I tried not to eat
cookies, cakes, pies,
ice cream, potato chips, pizza
but they tasted wonderful.
I couldn't always resist.
I was weak.

When I was 33 I was extremely depressed.
I started going to the gym with the goal
of losing weight.
I stopped eating the bad foods
and ate only the good foods.
I stopped eating meat.
I worked out.
I lost weight.
Cookies, cakes, pies, ice cream, potato chips, pizza
did not pass my lips.
I ate
apples, bananas, peaches, pears, yogurt,
brussel sprouts, broccoli, peas, carrots, celery.
1200 calories a day.
Less than 10 grams of fat a day.
50 pounds vanished from my body.

For the first time in my life
I was a thin person.
I had muscle tone.
I was fit.
Shopping was fun.
I looked great.
Guys at work who had never talked to me before
started talking to me.
People looked at me differently.
People treated me differently.

People were happy for me.
Inside, I was the same person.
I was tired and sore.
I was not as strong as I thought someone
who works out all the time should be.
How I looked became an obsession.
My everyday thoughts swirled around gaining weight.
After five years of a highly restrictive diet,
my body rebelled.
I stopped exercising.
The 50 pounds came back
and so did another 50.

Now, I eat the foods I like.
I should exercise but I don't.
My doctor worries about my weight.
I am on high-cholesterol medication.
I am happy.
I know my weight is not healthy
but I don't hate myself.
I went to college and earned a
Bachelor's degree.
I am earning a second master's degree.
I founded and manage a nonprofit journalism program for college students.
I try to make the world a better place.

When people see me, the first thing they see is a fat person.

I no longer absorb their judgment.

▶ Dawn Heinbach holds an M.A. in Publishing from Rosemont College and is completing a master's degree in journalism at New York University. In 2016, her poem "Stunning" earned an award from the English department at Kutztown University of Pennsylvania. In 2015, Heinbach founded Writing Wrongs, a 501(c)(3) nonprofit that facilitates a literary journalism program for college students. She lives in Berks County with her partner of 25 years and their two rescue cats..

Veiled

By Joan Zachary

JOAN ZACHARY moved to Pennsylvania in 1974. She has been intrigued by photography since childhood, but she is also a musician and writer. Currently Joan lives in Point Phillips, Pennsylvania with her fiancé, musician Randall Smith, one very photogenic cat, and the many residents of Plastiqueville.

We're All In A Box: Reflections on Embracing One's True (Queer) Self

By Rachel C. Thompson

I have a few problems with identity, identity politics, and how others perceive each other based on shallow ideas about identity. These ideas, of course, comes out of media and not reality or anyone's critical thinking skills. Reality is wide and deep and thus boring from the media's sensationalist point of view. Media promotes conflict, i.e. produces stories, and will create trouble where none exists. Identity is one of the ways media and politics yank our collective cranks.

Identity is mostly about what one does, according to common discourse. Bob's a fireman, for example. Thus, I am a lot of things. I hold many identities and they were all perfectly fine—praises heaped on me for them— until I made one identity change in my life. Not really a change, more an openly shared self-discovery.

I stopped fighting myself and "came out." I'm queer and that surprised everyone I worked hard to fool, but I worked hardest to fool myself. I worked hardest to fit into the concept of identity that others wanted me to be.

What was I before I came out at age 35? A lot of things. Artist, musician, writer, construction manager, expert in several fields, antique motorcycle geek, nerd of many scholarly interests, long distance runner, parent, divorcée, single parent, bi-polar, and much more. These were all perfectly fine when I wasn't queer. (I've always been queer, just didn't know it.)

Now, I don't fit anywhere.

My identities were all supplanted by secrets. I revealed these secrets in order to save my own life. I am still all the things I ever was. The biggest and only real change was when I became honest to myself.

Everything the rest of what the world saw in me beforehand has not changed, but everyone and everything changed around me. The price I paid to be free of inner torment cost me my entire world. I lost everything, home, profession, family and children. My former world was crushed, destroyed, and made no more—a dead parakeet inside a cage. To quote Joe Walsh, "Everybody's so different; I haven't changed."

Coming out at age 35, in the mid-90s, was hard. I fought my entire life to stuff down the queerness inside me. Why? To fit in, to be a good Catholic sheep, to avoid the ire of family and society—that wasn't all. I did not, could not face myself. I felt one way so I ran the other. My inner life did not match the identity imposed on me by culture. I did not understand my feelings. I had no words to describe them, and I had no way of understanding until I accessed the Internet. Meeting people like me online and knowing I wasn't alone, or crazy, or even unusual, turned my world inside out. All my expectations in life, the expectations that everyone had of me and for me, came down in an avalanche.

Where I grew up in the so called liberal Northeast, nothing was gay. There were no resources, no help, no questions asked, and nobody to ask anyway.

Everything under the rug, please. Wear that blanket of guilt and shame. It's a badge of honor.

In my day, I never met or knew a gay person that I recognized as gay. There was no mention of homosexuality or gender variations in high school sex education. Much later, I learned some folks I knew all my life are or were gay before passing. You didn't talk about that. It's a sin. It's the devil. It's not normal.

How do you fix gay? Those around me when I was younger would have said to go talk to the priest. Join the church and be a celibate servant. Or do missionary work. Be anything, do anything but don't be queer.

Thus, I was ill-prepared for what came next. Oh, I wasn't blind. I knew "coming out" was the end of my life. In fact, I tried suicide before coming out — seemed a reasonable solution at the time.

But my decisions were more complex than that. I have another identity. The other thing building steam in my mind's boiler since I was a kid is bipolar disorder. I'm mentally ill, but I'm not stupid. In fact, turns out quite the opposite. Unfortunately, "coming out" and my first very bad mental breakdowns came together, and as one may expect, that's not a good time. Losing everything in life will do that. It springs the coiled trap. Perhaps stuffing my real identity for half a lifetime is what caused panic attacks and depression, but I think not. These two problems did make it harder to cope. One bad identity, mentally ill, is enough to crush one under social ostracization's jackboot.

These two identities, queer and mentally ill, led the courts to take my parental rights away. It's different now, but in 1995 denying me access to my own daughter — due to being queer, not mentally ill — was perfectly legal and the usual treatment. Queer parents must go.

"But I'm the same person!"

Not in the eyes of the law then, or in anyone else's eyes for that matter.

It takes money to fight the system. I didn't have any, too busy being homeless, chronically unemployed, on welfare, and facing one disaster after the next between spending time in mental hospitals. It's hard—going from a big "McMansion" to living in a car. I fought the courts without a lawyer. My unstable life did not improve my chances of seeing my daughter.

Desperation twists the brain into survival mode and you lose the ability to fight or even stand.

Years went by, I got back on my feet, but too late. I lost my daughter. She has nothing to do with me. I suspect it's because the courts and my ex hung negative identity handles on me for so long. But on the other hand, my child from my first marriage never had a problem with me coming out. Funny, kids can be happy to love their gay parents. Who knew? I didn't.

Of course, I didn't take this lying down. I fought. Another of my identities

Identities Kill

When I came out, no one could have been more shocked than I. Raised on 1950s perceptions of gay— my parents' perceptions, not mine— I had been manhandled into false ideals about gay identity. The concepts implanted upon me were my mother's, who I learned much later had a few gay man buddies. Mom's idea, direct from church propaganda, was that being gay is a dirty, best left secret, sinful, perverted and damned state of being. By the way, she was a progressive liberal.

When I learned that all this negative social misinformation is based on bullshit and that there is an actual community of people like me, I was shocked. I had no idea.

The GLBT community is, as it turns out, a wide and deep community with churches, social clubs, long term partnerships, gay families with children and much, much more. All of that culture was underground until recently, but my new community always existed, like-minded people do congregate. I didn't know any of that and what a delightful surprise to learn I wasn't going to Hell alone. (Although now, I no longer believe in gods or devils.) Holy crap, the GLBT community is just people! Not the fearful 'other' I'm supposed to run from and hate and kill and destroy.

I now understand the folly of Mom's worldview. I found out later what hurtful results of her mentality and others like her are. Gay teens are still regularly kicked out of homes and worse. Mom's identity concepts inadvertently killed her gay friend, Mr. Wagner, which is a good example of how identities kill.

Her super Catholicism drove her to try and save her friend. It's the modern Spanish Inquisition—if you can't burn the body, torture the mind. The Inquisitors were, after all, saving souls, too.

Long story short, on the day Wagner committed suicide, he called Mom and asked her to come over right away. His intent was that she would find him with his brains blown out. His suicide note said that and gave further reasons as to why he did it such as his guilt over being gay and unable to change. He needed to end the pain. But also, he wanted to show Mom the result of her great guilt on him. He wanted her to find his body.

So much for Mom's failed but self-justified way of helping to change another's label and provide a new, fresh, clean, acceptable identity because anything's better than being gay. She pushed her answer to the gay problem in my youth which was all I ever knew about it.

"One should join the priesthood or become a nun," Mom repeated the 1950s way of dealing with queers. "If you can't stop it, stuff it."

Mom's typical way of fixing gay killed Mr. Wagner. This shit still happens today.

Mom's goal was saving his soul, but rather she guilted him into a dramatic suicide whereby, according to her faith, suicide disallowed Wagner's entry into heaven. She had taken that away from him.

By the way, Mom didn't see the body, only the note. She didn't feel guilty doing God's work. Ironic as Hell, isn't it? "What so ever you do…"

Labels and identities imposed on the 'other' are bundles of shallow fears posing as reality, and as such, dangerous. But not just dangerous to us queer folk. Separating out and mischaracterizing any community for the sake of fear-mongering social controls, advancing politics or profits, hurts the whole. Each aspect of humanity is a part of the whole. A society made into Swiss cheese by cutting out the most fabulous parts loses its ability to stand unified.

I think the world would have been much better off had Mr. Wagner told Mom to go fuck herself.

He was an interesting, intelligent, worldly man with a lot to offer. I was only a teen, but had he lived he might have been a great help to me. Had I known he was gay, ditto. He was a nice man and very kind to me.

If you ask me how I'd identify him, I'd answer, "Nice man."

came into play. I'm a fighter. But after ten years, I lost the legal fight anyway. Daughter gained the age of consent and she didn't consent to seeing me. So, I guess add loser to my list of identities. Oh, but I wasn't done.

I started another new identity after being beat up by the Allentown, Pa., police for being in distress with a panic attack. I was a queer living in a slum on welfare. This experience prompted a new identity: activist. For the next ten years, I fought the system while I fought for my own survival. I worked for human rights, gay rights, people's rights to be people. The cops punched, kicked, and spit on me so I punched back— metaphorically.

I've collected so many new identities since coming out as queer: activist, agitator, writer, protester, lobbyist, organizer, speaker, and while I was at it, I also got more involved in the straight world through the arts. I mixed myself into many social things that I could not do before allowing myself to be me. I became a better person for owning up to the hated moniker called queer.

Oh, but I'm not done with identities. I have another one now: "old lady." I moved to the Deep South because it's cheap. I'm disabled (long story, maybe I'll tell you another day.) Here I'm not a gay person, that's too dangerous. I never speak of it. My partner and I never give any indication we are a couple. It's 1960 here, you don't talk about it. Our neighbors whisper about the two ladies while freely spewing right wing bullshit and hallelujah religion. I listen and nod. I try not to comment.

I avoid most people although I am involved in the little community where I live. My new identity is clubhouse volunteer, library volunteer, writer's group member, author, musician, just plain Jane and a nice, good old neighbor, the kind that will do anything for you.

Why I put on this other identity here is to prevent finding myself hanging from a tree by my neck. Hiding inside the herd works. I pretend to be just like them. Some here think I'm a smarty pants. I'm educated and articulate and some folks around here don't cotton to that. But it's fine, I can and do blend in anywhere because I have a weapon called common ground.

Some think or suspect I'm a liberal, or a libertarian, or Christian. I'm not. I'm realistic. I don't hold to ideologies in general as I see them as intellectually lazy. I can and do speak their language, however. Add social chameleon to my list of identifiers. Add critical thinker, too, but don't say that where I live—Fox News is the big religion here, telling folks to be afraid of intellect, and science, and facts, and Blacks and…it's a long list and I'm on it. Probably for more than one reason.

So, what am I now? I am none of the things I've done or do, and the list is longer than seen above. What do I make of myself? What do you make of me? It doesn't matter. What one pigeon-holes me with is inadequate, there isn't a container big enough to host all my nouns and adjectives. What do you think of this queer now?

Have you suffered a lot? Me, too!

Can you identify with any of my identity handles? I bet you can. I've hunted, camped, owned boats, and fished. I've worked on my own cars so add handy and outdoorsy. I read a lot, how about you?

I bet we have more in common than differences. Like movies? Are you a veteran? Wow, me, too! I have even more. Near death survivor. Cancer

Rachel C. Thompson, *U-Hall*, 2005

patient caregiver. Maybe I'm more like you than you're comfortable admitting. Maybe I've done more in my life than you, oops, most people think that's a problem. I may even remind you of some aspect of yourself that you'd rather not face.

The fact that I faced my monsters doesn't go over well with people who have not, or will not. But at the end of the day what am I? I'm not a what. I'm a who.

Identity politics makes me into a what, a thing, not a person. I am one speck in a huge box with copious room. I really only fit into one identity box. It's the same one you're in. We're in this life together like it or not. We share the same label, it's called human being. To hate me for what you perceive I am is to hate that part yourself.

"Whatsoever you do to the least of my brothers, that you do unto me."
Take a wild guess who said that.
Do you identify with that character? If so, do you show it?
Love thy neighbor, or at least leave us queers alone.

▶ Rachel C. Thompson, former freelance writer, wrote and cartooned for magazines and newspapers (such as the now defunct Lehigh Valley News Group) from the Lehigh Valley, Pennsylvania. before moving to Florida. To date, she self-published four novels and one anthology. Nonfiction credits include press releases, ad-copy and other materials for nonprofit organizations. From sci-fi and fantasy, to social satire and historical fiction, Thompson twists it all.

Invisible

By Tiffani Burnett Velez

When I was a child, I remember playing that game we all play when we ask ourselves what super power we'd have if we could have one. Being an introvert, I always thought being invisible was a good choice. In my adulthood, I learned that invisibility is not always a good thing.

I was paralyzed by the time I was 21 years old. I was also pregnant with my first child and newly married. It happened, almost, overnight. Three weeks earlier, I had been walking around, driving more than an hour to work in the heavily populated King of Prussia area, and traveling in and out of Center City Philadelphia to file suits at various courthouses against delinquent clients for my employer. It was a horrible job, and I was paid only $8.50 an hour for it, and even though my title was "Collections Manager," I had no direct reports and the only thing I was managing was the continuous filling up of my gas tank.

I worked for a small technology company, and it was the early days of cellphones and contracts that never seemed to end. As the "collections manager," my job was to collect unpaid bills from customers with fake IDs. To this day, I have no idea why any employer would create a budget for a job like this, but not everyone is a genius either. I was moving along, doing my pointless job diligently when, like that, in the snap of a finger, I started to feel an annoying numbness crawling up my legs and then my arms. No matter what I did, sink my feet into scalding hot bath water, layer them with two and three pairs of wool socks, stab them with a pencil, etc. I could not conjure up any feeling from my ankles to my toes. Within another week, the numbness had ascended to my knees, and then my chest, and I could no longer breathe.

My husband, Leonardo, and I hadn't even been married six months yet, and here he was driving me in various snowstorms and bad weather from doctor to doctor. He was, naturally, scared and confused; 21-year-olds aren't supposed to have, as one ER respiratory therapist said of me, "breathing problems like an 80-year-old lady." Leonardo's biggest concerns were whether or not I would survive and if our child would make it into the world.

I went from hospital emergency room to hospital emergency room, but I kept getting turned away, being told that I was "just anxious about being pregnant" or "nervous about the newlywed life." In other words, because I was a woman and dealing with the hormones of pregnancy, I must have been just going a little insane. I was the cause of my suffocation and paralysis, I was being told. It couldn't possibly be *a disease* that was taking my life from me and threatening my unborn child's life, too. Naturally, I must have been conjuring this all up from the power of my own depraved feminine mind.

I had to sleep sitting up, because if I laid down, I went blue. I couldn't use my diaphragm anymore. Soon, I couldn't walk without assistance. I was asphyxiating just riding in the passenger seat of my car while my husband drove through the blizzard of 1996 to get me into an emergency room that would not turn me away. I was finally rescued by a family friend who was a nurse and had worked in a neurologist's office for many years. She was now stationed at the county prison, a job she abandoned for a couple days to accompany me to the ER.

"I've seen this before," she said, "when I was a nurse in Philadelphia. There is something very wrong with your nervous system."

It was flu season and every bed in the hospital was taken up with sick, coughing people. I was wheeled into the hallway and left there, the color fast fading from my face with the lack of oxygen. My friend refused to leave my side, demanding that doctors finally take a real look at me. An Ob-Gyn eventually agreed that there was more than one life to be concerned with here, and insisted that admitting me would be best for everyone. When a neurologist was called from his deep sleep at home to come and assess me, he declared that I had either Multiple Sclerosis, Lyme Disease, or something called Guillain-Barre Syndrome (an extremely rare autoimmune disease that attacks the nervous system and causes varying degrees of paralysis).

It turned out, I had something even worse, but this was the first time I was getting any meaningful attention. No one was calling me "anxious" anymore. Though, honestly, when the entire medical establishment in your community refuses to save your life, because you're a woman with a medical mystery they're too lazy to solve, it can get stressful. Still, I remained the calmest person in the situation. I had hope that everything would work out. My doctors were stressed, my new husband was terrified, my parents were baffled and depressed, my grandmother called every morning to check on me until I could no longer talk, because all the muscles in my face had collapsed.

Within 24 hours, I was flown to Philadelphia and my new neurologist was the same neurologist assigned to all US presidents. Dr. Robert Schwartman. I finally had good care. What he discovered was an extremely rare combination of Guillain-Barre Syndrome and Myasthenia Gravis (another rare neuromuscular disease). Though, at that time, I had not been diagnosed with the latter, only the former with a question mark added. There was something more to my body's self-destruction that even my brilliant doctor couldn't quite put his finger on. He needed more time than my weak insurance was willing to give me. In the span of my three week hospital stay, I was fired for being sick and not being able to return within two weeks, and my insurance dropped me before I had even gained the ability to walk again. I had to teach myself all over, at home, alone all day at my in-laws' house. At one point in the hospital, my physical therapist, a Holocaust survivor, helped me move 10 paces from the door of my room to the window.

She made me look out over the city of Philadelphia and said, "Remember this moment. This is the moment you became someone new. The girl who ran around before GBS is not the same girl who will learn a whole new way of movement. She's a woman and she's much stronger than the girl."

I had had five rounds of plasma exchange, and I was slated for five rounds of IVIG (intravenous immunoglobulin) when all my medical treatment was dropped and I was informed that, as a pregnant woman, I had racked up a more than $67,000 a day bill. My new husband and I filed for bankruptcy within two years. How were two college students, now with a baby, supposed to clear up such debt? No one cared. People at the church my husband had attended most of his life told him that we were sinners filing for bankruptcy. Everyone knows God loves two things: a cheerful giver to the church and someone with a high credit score. You have something under 600 and you're not getting into heaven.

I was already an unpopular face there, with my Jewish father and my quasi-Catholic upbringing with my mother and stepfather. My ideas were not exactly fundamentalist, or even Christian all the time, and in a denomination where faith is a mile wide and an inch deep, people expected me to be "healed" immediately or I must have been a bigger sinner than they already thought.

Eventually, I could walk again. It took about three months, and I returned to work at a different job. My baby grew strong and healthy, but my fatigue lingered. Some days, I was okay, but for weeks at a time, I would become so weak I had trouble using my neck and eyes. My breathing was occasionally weird, too, but having been separated from my last neurologist by, yet another, insurance company, I was seeing new people who insisted on the single GBS diagnosis, and since it is a disease that does not return, I was expected to get on with life without complaint or trouble.

My first baby was born, healthy and full term, in September 1996. Leonardo and I went on to have three more children. I had a minor relapse of MG with our second child, Isaac, though doctors in the Lehigh Valley did not recognize the disease. I had a major kidney issue with our daughter, and had kidney surgery while pregnant with her, and residual weakness after the birth of our youngest child (in 2004), but nothing as bad as the first time.

Anytime I got a cold, or bronchitis (which I acquired 10 different times in one year), I was sent home and told that I was just stressed. This time, I was conjuring up illnesses because I was the mother of three young children, and I didn't have enough education to be legitimately ill. I took that time to get accepted to Harvard University and returned to school. This is just when online education was making its debut. I figured this would help my case, that it would get me the healthcare I deserved. However, whenever I was ill, it was my fault that my immune system failed. For several years, I simply endured pneumonia, chronic tonsillitis, constant severe ear infections, and continued to accept that, because I was a woman, I was responsible for whatever ailment I experienced.

In the fall of 2002, I was experiencing a period of relatively good health, and I had landed a great job at Ralph Lauren for Macy's. I loved my job, and I was even promoted to a supervisory position there. However, my mystery illness returned, and I was unable to walk or sit up for more than 10 minutes at a time. My muscles were the weakest they had been since I'd first entered the hospital in Philadelphia six years prior. But this time, I was sent to a local neurologist who almost immediately diagnosed me with Multiple Sclerosis. It made sense. Mostly anyway. I had had one abnormal lumbar puncture (spinal tap) in 1996, I had all the symptoms. And even though all my tests were negative, the doctor continued with his diagnosis. I had a nagging feeling I should go back into the city for testing, but I was sick of the hunt and simply stuck with a doctor who didn't insult me. This was a mistake.

Within three years, my new neurologist had given me more than 10 rounds of 3,000 milligrams of IV steroids, pumped me full of beta interferons, and muscle relaxants, and had forced me into the MRI machine more than 15 times. The continued tests for MS were all negative, but the medications were making me deathly ill. I was experiencing the same breathing problems as I had all those years before. This time, I stopped the meds and didn't tell the doctor. I wanted to see what might happen if I defied him and charted my course. After all, nothing traditional medicine had done so far was working.

I pushed back. I told the neurologist I knew I didn't have MS, that this was something else and his medications were making me sick. He told me I was crazy and diagnosed me with Conversion Disorder, a disease that causes the nervous system to misinterpret stress as a physical attack and the body, essentially, attacks itself. It sounded plausible with this definition, but the definition at the time was one that defined the disease as being purely emotional, a mood disorder, a personality disorder mostly ascribed to women. Once again, I was being blamed for the illness I had acquired somewhere, somehow. I reported him to my insurance company who chased him out of the state, but I was terrified of what would happen to me if I didn't get the care I desperately needed.

I rejected his diagnosis, as did my primary physician who sent me to a new neurologist. I had little hope, but I tried to believe. I tried to have faith that I would one day be well, that someone would figure out what was wrong with my body.

This neurologist didn't have a clue what was going on with me and didn't pretend to. He did discover, however, that I suffered from severe chronic anemia, for which I received infusions of iron and shots of vitamin B12. He also sent me to a neuro ophthalmologist, because I had very specific vision complaints. That doctor suggested I see a specialized neurologist in Philadelphia for a test that looked for another very rare disease called Myasthenia Gravis. That test was borderline, but that inquiry sent me to a thoracic surgeon who tested me for thymic hyperplasia, an enlarged thymus gland which is extremely suspect for Myasthenia Gravis. Finally, people were listening.

Leonardo, and the children, took everything in stride. At times, it was stressful for them to see me using a cane or a wheelchair. Naturally, they worried about me. However, I managed to do all the things I ever wanted to do, despite my disability. I would hope that their lives were better than they could have been if I had been even worse.

In October 2013, I had my thymus gland removed, and I have seen a gradual improvement of my health ever since. My current neurologist, the one who had diagnosed my anemia, still waffles on my diagnosis, because I have fatigue at times. Though, I don't see these bouts as something as serious as he does, I agree that they are annoying and do take away whole days and weeks of my life. But I no longer walk with a cane (unless I am hiking) and I no longer use my wheelchair (unless I let someone else borrow it for some reason). I am much healthier than I have ever been, and I believe in my own gut feelings about my health.

Throughout this entire journey, I have learned that being a woman is one of my greatest strengths and hazards. I have also learned that, as a person with a disability, it is my job to advocate for myself, to speak my truth, and to listen to my body when it is telling me that I am doing way too much, because a person with an autoimmune disease is often invisible. We aren't seen or heard unless we are in a very serious situation, and even then, we're often ignored for the obvious. Doctors can be lazy and nearsighted, too. They can be selfish and narcissistic. Laying in my hospital bed, completely paralyzed, I listened to doctors talk about me like I wasn't there. One lamented that my illness wasn't "interesting enough" for him to waste his time on.

Recently, I was offered a fantastic position as an advocate for children with disabilities, with a well-known/well-respected disability nonprofit. Unfortunately, I sat most of the day and stared at a computer screen. Because Myasthenia Gravis affects my vision and eye muscles, and repetitive usage makes them weaken, by mid-day, I was having trouble seeing. I had also developed some issues with hearing and balance and had to leave that job after just two weeks. I have gone to eye doctors for years who, upon learning of my MG diagnosis, dismiss me and won't treat me because of it. I even had one doctor refuse to do a glaucoma test on me, because my eye muscles were too weak.

Shortly thereafter, I was also offered a position as a program director of an ESL department at a small technical college. I was thrilled, but once again, my invisible illness broke through. The one hour drive each way was becoming impossible, because I simply couldn't see. I've worn glasses for years, but I dreaded going back to an eye doctor and getting dismissed, having to hold all the symptoms of my illness alone. As fate would have it, on my way out of Costco on a Sunday afternoon, I ran over to the optical center and begged for an appointment. The doctor got me in and she immediately asked, "How have you been functioning all these years? You cannot legally drive without glasses, not even during the day!"

She then proceeded to give me the best advice I've ever gotten regarding eye issues and MG. She said, "Trust yourself and demand quality healthcare, because bad healthcare doesn't help anyone. What you've experienced is egregious."

I said, "Well, I'm a woman and we're taught to be polite and invisible, aren't we?"

She leaned in close. "Excuse my French, but f that," she said. "You deserve better. We all do."

I know that more than one person reading this can relate. Those of us who have to draw up special efforts just to function as others effortlessly do, understand what it means to have accommodation; we know the infinite value of it. We also know what it means to be invisible. People see us when they want to and they see our difference when they want to. It would be great to be fully seen, fully respected, and fully equal.

Why Tiffani chose to write this: She chose to write about living with a disability, because the largest minority in the United States is made up of differently abled people — people who use assistive devices to use their senses, to use their limbs, to make the world a more accessible place to them. Frequently, Tiffani uses a cane, and when very weak, a wheelchair. She wears corrective lenses at all times, and she uses text to speech software when her voice is too weak to speak. Despite the differences she lives with, she continues to demand more opportunities for success and independence.

▶ Tiffani Burnett Velez is the author of four novels and one nonfiction book. She is a professor of English at a local community college and the program director of the English language program at a technical school. She lives in Eastern Pennsylvania with her family..

My Daily Agenda

By Thurston D. Gill Jr.

I look at my daily agenda as a culmination of my conscious and subconscious objectives for my day.

I shake my head when I seriously evaluate my to-do-list.

Top of the List:
The things that feed my feelings for satisfaction.

Bottom of the List
The things that feed my spirit and renew my mind.

▶ Thurston D. Gill Jr. went from law enforcement to various aspects of the security industry: healthcare & campus security, loss prevention, a private security contractor, and security training & development management. He was ordained as a minister more than 30 years ago and invested several years of life as a mental health recovery specialist and an intensive case manager.

Purging DNA

By Dawn Heinbach

There is a lot of talk about violence these days. Violence against women: sexual assault, domestic violence. Gun violence. Verbal and physical assault. Child abuse. Parents murdering children. Children murdering children.

We talk about ending the violence. We want it to stop. We look for people to blame, for causes and solutions. We hold meetings and rallies. We hold signs and march.

The world is a violent place. It always has been. Mother Nature is wondrous, spectacular, awe-inspiring, life-giving—but she has a twisted sense of humor. Standing back admiring her work, she realized something was missing. Let's make this interesting, she said, and added the statute that some species must die so that others may live. Mother Nature is the ultimate "Mommy Dearest."

The orca grabs the seal pup's tail in its teeth and flips it into the air. Another orca catches it. They toss the pup back and forth, using the baby as a toy. Eventually, they rip it apart. Back on the shore, there is one mother who is now childless.

Man's arrival did not curb the violence but added to it. Early *homo sapiens* defended their territory, their food stores against other groups who invaded them. They fought fatal battles wielding clubs and pointed sticks. Most anything can be a weapon. Heads were smashed on rocks, brains expelled. Muscles and tissue were pierced. Blood flowed. Men, women, and children.

You would think that after all these years of evolution, we would advance. Our compassion would overcome our need to dominate. We would develop more empathy. Some people have reached this state, but the majority are still Neanderthals.

A gray squirrel climbs up a tree to where a sparrow's brood nest holds three two-day-old chicks. It kills and eats two of them. Sated but opportunistic, the squirrel grabs the third chick in its mouth and carries it off. The parents' lives are turned upside down as they sit on a branch and wonder what they're supposed to do now.

Sometimes we think we can kill nicely, that this makes us more civilized than our furred and feathered counterparts. The electric chair was one of the first ways we deemed acceptable for killing criminals. It's supposed to be painless, but things can and do go wrong—accidentally or purposely. As the electricity runs through your body, your bowels and bladder may empty. You might convulse. You are not aware of your body's response, but it's not dignified, especially when people are watching.

We moved on to gas. You are unconscious at the time of death, but before that, you will see the gas as the pellets dissolve. You are aware that death is eminent. Again, you might urinate or shit your pants, or vomit. Gas chambers are expensive, so this method didn't seep into all of society's crevices. Money takes precedent over humaneness.

Lethal injection is the kindest way to die. The sodium thiopental makes you completely unconscious so that you can't feel your lungs unable to expand when the pancuronium bromide paralyzes your muscles. When they inject the potassium chloride, you don't feel the intense pain of your heart ceasing to pump, stopping the blood flow to your organs. Yes, this is the kindest way to kill.

The red-tailed hawk swoops down and catches the yellow-bellied woodpecker in one swift motion. It doesn't even cease flight. As it carries off the screaming, flapping bird, the hawk pushes its long, sharp talons into the woodpecker's chest.

Teenagers have entered the fight against violence. They say that too many of them are being killed in schools. They don't want to die where they go to learn. Their bodies are riddled with bullets from AR-15 rifles. When these bullets hit them, the teenagers have pain. They gasp for breath when their lungs are pierced. The bullets swirl through their bodies and rip apart their hearts, livers, kidneys. Blood stops flowing, pools in cavities as their organs fail. The teenagers say they want to live.

A red fox lays low in the brush, watching as a doe gives birth. When the fawn has fully entered its new world, the fox darts in and grabs it. The frantic mother follows the fox, snorting and stomping her feet, as it carries her baby off to feed its own kits.

▶ Dawn Heinbach holds an M.A. in Publishing from Rosemont College and is completing a master's degree in journalism at New York University. In 2016, her poem "Stunning" earned an award from the English department at Kutztown University of Pennsylvania. In 2015, Heinbach founded Writing Wrongs, a 501(c)(3) nonprofit that facilitates a literary journalism program for college students. She lives in Berks County with her partner of 25 years and their two rescue cats..

On Work and Wealth:
Neither of These Should Define Us

By Angel R. Ackerman

I find myself the exception versus the norm on just about every issue out there. I have a disability, so movement is not a natural event for me. It requires focus and concentration and decisions every time I walk, every time I work out. And it involves more than my fair share of falling down.

My parents are high school drop outs. My mom is super-intelligent with words but terrified of fractions, so she never got her GED. My dad could win games of chess, took things apart and put them back together, and had a mind capable of seeing ideas and solutions that I can't.

My extended family struggles with addiction and substance abuse. Wedding receptions often become brawls and funerals usually end in the bar across the street.

None of this bothers me. I have accepted these facts about myself and my history without an issue, and most people can hear them with an attempt at empathy or congratulate me on everything I have achieved.

Because if there is one person that should be a statistic it's me.

I should be dead—because the doctors said I should have died when I was born premature and my lungs collapsed twice. I should be dead—because with my family history I should have been attached to a bottle and perhaps killed myself and others in a DUI-caused accident or died in an accident when family members drove me home along that windy River Road under the influence.

My family had struggles, and here I was the kid the doctors said would never walk or talk or live.

But I did.

My family couldn't help me decide where to go to college, high school teachers did.

My family couldn't afford the study abroad that would have allowed me to finish my French degree the way the college wanted.

I don't think anyone in my life, my neighborhood or my circles judge me on these facts.

But I have noticed one tendency of American society: to judge socio-economic status and employment.

And it's a crisis, in my eyes.

I currently work in a clothing warehouse, for a company rated one of the best places to work in the Lehigh Valley. I make the same amount of money I made working for a local nonprofit, in a position people were often impressed to hear about. But that position in fundraising was high stress and the workplace was toxic, so I praised the pandemic as it closed life down and allowed me to catch my breath. That employer fired me, and I was relieved to be free.

But traditional America does not like poor people and it judges people on their employment.

So when I took the job in the warehouse, at a company I selected based on how it treats their workers and on their mission, I got the vibe that people felt sorry for me. It's not an unfamiliar feeling. I worked at Target for almost 10 years, because I found part-time professional employment in my field—journalism—non-existent unless you wanted to freelance and hustle for income. And part-time employment in nonprofits, while meaningful and dynamic, led to part-time money and full-time stress. I had one boss who called me at home when I was teaching my daughter to ride a bicycle because she couldn't figure out how to download a PDF I had sent and reattach it to an email for the printer.

I worked at Target because, unlike journalism and nonprofit management, Target respected my wish to pursue more education (I was working on a second bachelors in International Affairs and later a masters in world history at West Chester University 90 minutes away). Target allowed me the part-time evening scheduling I needed if I wanted to be present to raise my daughter.

Now every family is different, and some families use day care or nannies or arrangements with neighbors as a network for the safety and upbringing of their children, but I knew when I left the journalism industry that I wanted to be there for my daughter.

In making that choice, I sacrificed my own career, especially with the decline of print journalism. I watched my colleagues get laid off and struggle to find new jobs. By then my daughter was five, and that second bachelors I mentioned? I enrolled at Lafayette College with two hopes: to gain credentials for my knowledge gained from the journalism industry and to set a good example for my kindergartner that education offered opportunity.

But my friends, my peers and supervisors at Target, and most certainly the Target shoppers constantly judged me. Many of my Target co-workers thought I was too smart and that my approaches to tasks stemmed from an air of superiority. So many people yelled at me and berated me and took their frustrations out on me during those ten years.

Yet, at the same time, when a job required a certain educated intelligence, like overseeing the supply order for the commercial kitchen, enforcing food safety or counting money and logging paperwork in the cash office, my background and skills were welcomed.

I should never have to feel embarrassed because I work in a warehouse, and it's uncomfortable to see supervisors suddenly realize how smart you are, because even they had a notion of who you are based on the job you chose to do.

The Wawa cashiers, pizza delivery drivers, house cleaners, baristas, waitresses, car detailers, factory workers, bartenders and every other so-called unskilled laborer out there does an important job that contributes something to all of our lives and to our society at large.

And too often Americans don't give other Americans a chance because of some preconceived notion that correlates socio-economic status and/or profession with worthiness or intelligence. Sometimes life choices-- which include what we do for a living and the type of work we do-- are deliberate and sometimes they are desperate. But that doesn't mean the person who makes these choices is less of a person or less valuable.

Some people in less respected positions have no other options. Sometimes their life experience leaves them without the information needed to move in another direction. These people may need advice or assistance or well-meaning intervention, but sometimes they don't. Sometimes, the overqualified person would rather do a job that offers them scheduling flexibility or less stress. Sometimes these jobs can make more of a difference in the world than more career-oriented positions.

I currently work in a warehouse.

I have worked in nonprofit development and communications.

I worked as a journalist for 15 years.

I am a novelist.

I founded my own publishing company.

I worked in the café at Target for almost 10 years.

I am a mom.

I even did a stint as a writer in a rubber/plastic company.

I have volunteered at the library, 4H, Girl Scouts.

I have helped a budding anti-human trafficking nonprofit with annual reports and press releases.

I have mentored college students and other writers.

I have led writers groups and critique groups.

I even served on the board of the Penn State University Cooperative Extension of Northampton County, where my Slate Belt rural heritage and my current urban lifestyle met.

I foster cats.

So don't make me feel insignificant because I value my quality of life over my career. Don't make me feel like less of a person because my house is small, because it is enough for me. I don't care how much money you make, or how hard you work. Life is just too short.

▶ Angel R. Ackerman had a 15-year career in print journalism and has dabbled in creative and travel writing. Her Fashion and Fiends novels are available through Parisian Phoenix. Her non-journalism work has been featured in *Dime Store Review*'s 10-word stories, *StepAway Magazine*, *Rum Punch Press*, *Global Studies South*, *Hippocampus Magazine*, The Mighty, Yahoo News and the *SAGE Encyclopedia of Poverty*. Her portfolio and web site is angelackerman.com.

Maryann Riker, *We are...*

▶ Mixed-media artist Maryann J. Riker uses handmade paper, book board, book cloth, beading, paint, embroidery and transparencies to convey a visual narrative through the book format. Riker holds a B.A. from Moravian College, an M.A. degree from Montclair State University and an MFA degree from Vermont College.

Secrets From the Steelworker's Daughter:

GROWING UP "PA. DUTCH" IN WORKING CLASS SOUTH BETHLEHEM

By Gayle F. Hendricks

I don't think about identity. Or race. Or gender. Or any of the other big topics in today's world. Because when I do, I struggle with them. I don't know what the answers are or how to even answer the questions.

The struggle is real. What is my identity?

Things I know for sure: I am human. I am female. I am a steelworker's daughter. I am an environmentalist and a feminist. I am an American. And a pacifist. Those are all facts that can be confirmed either biologically or sociologically. I like that everything else is kind of gray. But sometimes I'm jealous of other people that have clear identities.

I hear friends and colleagues and people on TV or what-not, talking about their identity and their culture. And I keep saying to myself, what do I have to fill in those blanks? I have yet to come up with anything.

Historically, my ancestors came from Germany, and they settled in Pennsylvania. In many ways my heritage, my culture, would be Pennsylvania German/Dutch/Deutsch. We never really talk about that in the family. My mother had a few Pennsylvania German traditions that she followed — sauerkraut on New Year's Day, eating something green on Maundy Thursday, making fastnachts, a pickle in the Christmas tree—but that's about it. Nobody I knew spoke German or the Pennsylvania Dutch dialect, no one participated in German events or celebrations. My family assimilated because that's what you did. I'm not even sure when my family came to America. We didn't talk about it. My maternal great-great grandfather was born in America in 1867. His father fought in the Civil War. There was some skeleton in the closet about someone named Charles and he was a junk man.

In my forties, I was into genealogy—well I still am, but I suck at it—and I went through microfiche of the *Daily Times* (precursor of the Bethlehem *Globe Times*, you know, the newspaper) to see if I could solve the mystery.

January 9, 1885.

I came up with a series of stories fit for a New York City tabloid. They were salacious. "A Father's Awful Crime," "An Old Story of a Murdered Peddler Revived," and "Louis Carl, the Murderer, Arrested." Not one single elder person in my family would confirm nor deny that this was the "junk-man" of the scandal my mother wouldn't tell me about. Louis Carl was a criminal. Now none of them are left so I'll never know unless academic genealogist Louis Henry Gates puts a team of researchers on the mystery.

It all adds up. A peddler is a junk-man. And my mother's family is filled with drunks and abusers. My maternal grandfather was one of them. My father was just a drunk.

The ruins of the Bethlehem Steel blast furnace in south Bethlehem..

So where does that leave my cultural identity? I don't know.

My family and my extended family is large. As were most of my relatives. We multiplied like bunnies. And most of the extended family didn't have money. As my mother put it we didn't "have a pot to piss in." My mom was a homemaker like many women of her generation. My dad was a Union steelworker. Yes, with a capital U. He lived and breathed unions. Maybe that's the reason I don't like them. I saw how they screwed him over time and time again.

If they said strike, he went on strike. When there was long strike—I was told by my older siblings—there was very little food or money. My mother would have to get what she called "relief." I believe it's similar to what we call welfare today. My one sister talks about her relief glasses, and how ugly they were. I think my family got "relief" more often than my mother admitted.

When I heard about the wonderful salaries people made at the Steel, I wondered why my father didn't bring one of them home. We had a lot of people my family, and my father made very little. He worked in the blast furnace. He was always dirty. The neighborhood laundromat had a bank of machines that said "steel workers' clothes," so that you didn't ruin the other machines with the iron dust. We hung out all the clothes to dry, still do, and had to have them in by a certain time so when they reloaded the blast furnace … or whatever they did to the blast furnace and it sent out that huge plume of black smoke … it would not soil the clean laundry. We protected the clean laundry, but it didn't really matter that we were breathing the infamous black plume.

The going "joke" at my house was that my father did one shift at the Steel and a second drinking at the Democratic Club unless, of course, he was working a second job. These second jobs included picking peaches at Bechtold's Orchard and cleaning a ballet studio. He cleaned a ballet studio so my older siblings could take lessons. My mom made the costumes. He went to family events, if he wasn't working. I hated the years he worked day shift on Christmas morning. We'd have to wait until almost dinnertime to open presents. It took me until my teens to realize that Christmas was really just my mom doing her annual shopping for us. She was clever. We had a lot of kids in our family and we had to get new pajamas sometime.

We had one black and white television. In addition to soap operas and sitcoms, it played a whole lot of the civil rights and women's movement, Vietnam, and assassinations on the news.

The more I think about this, the more I realize that the tween/teen years were my wakeup time. So, those formative years from maybe eight or nine to Richard Nixon resigning in 1974 really made me who I am today. And that person was not male, white or rich.

The Vietnam War made me a pacifist. I don't thank vets for their service. They signed up for the military, it's their job. They knew the risks.

I was in second or third grade when Kennedy was killed. By 1968, we had race riots and assassinations or attempts on George Wallace, Bobby Kennedy, and Martin Luther King. Vietnam was the lead story on the news. Some days it seemed like the only story, only to be replaced in the 70s with Watergate.

I was a tween when I figured out that not only women weren't equal, neither were a lot of other people. I'm fairly sure that I thought slavery and inequity was in the past. I didn't grow up in the South and Jim Crow meant little to me. I guess I had on my rose-colored glasses. If I see it, I'm generally propelled into action. How could more than half the people —women and people of color — not be treated equally?

I think I was sheltered being a steelworker's daughter. I grew up in the late 50s and 60s in an ethnically diverse neighborhood. I was exposed to all kinds of people and all kinds of traditions. And if you looked up the word "melting pot" in a dictionary, there was South Bethlehem. As the settlers arrived each neighborhood settled together. Each neighborhood had their own identity and their own church — South Bethlehem is filled with steeples — and stores. When we shopped, we were instructed to go to the Portuguese tailor, the Polish butcher, etc. As time went by people started to ignore the divisions. I figured out much later was that our melting pot was mostly Eastern European, Russian, Italian, and Irish. People that fled their homelands in search of opportunity. They were "white." We didn't have the diversity that we call diversity today. There weren't, and still aren't, many people from Asia, the Middle East, and India. My mom grew up on Pawnee Street across the street from the c.1890 African Methodist Episcopal church.

I knew not all neighborhoods were like mine, but it took me a while to really figure out how and why. My aunt lived in East Orange, N.J., and we would go up there to visit her. Her neighborhood was majority Black, not ethnically-diverse, like my neighborhood was. Sure, I noticed it, but I didn't care. She was friends with all her neighbors. One day, I made the leap to knowing that there was something different here. She asked me to go to the grocery store, which was four or five blocks away from the house, on the main drag. I went to the grocery store, and I noticed that all the billboards and stuff on the street were the same as the ads that I was getting back at home. But they all had Black people on them. When I went into the store, I noticed the same thing that all the signage and stuff in the store featured

Black people. And, then and there I discovered targeted marketing.

It wasn't until I came out of the store that I realized that I was one of three white people on the street. It was unsettling that maybe there was a difference.

Later, maybe in the last thirty years, I discovered that not only was my grandfather a drunk and a wife beater, but he was a belonged The Improved Order of the Redmen. (Oppomanyhook Tribe, No. 302, Bethlehem, Pa.) a fraternal organization that had rituals and regalia that are modeled after Native Americans. But the members were all white men. I have a picture of him (left) dressed in all his wretched finery. He's even carrying a tomahawk. Looking around the greater Lehigh Valley there are many Redman Halls. I never gave them much thought. The group still exists but is it racist? By my definition probably yes.

Initially, my classes in school were more ethnically diverse than racially diverse. I can see that now. Grade school was fairly "ethnic white." Junior High School more diverse racially. High School the most diverse of all.

Of my friends, almost everybody's grandmother spoke a different language. But we shared one culture: food. When my mother was young, she got together with the neighbors and they all cooked. They learned from each other. In turn, our cuisine was from around the world. And if my mother didn't know the name of it, she would attach a name to it. Probably a phonetic guess. Today I'll go to a Russian bazaar or similar event and learn the real names of these ethnic dishes. But I still call it by the name my mother gave it.

The Pill was invented and the sexual repression of the 50s was vanishing. Women started breaking into traditional male occupations. The first woman in Congress was Jeannette Rankin (Republican, Montana). In 1955, when I was born, there were 15 women in Congress. By 1969, there were only 11.

And only one was Black: Shirley Chisholm (Democrat, New York). Although still heavily white and male, today Congress looks representative of America with more members who are Hispanic/Latinx, Indigenous/Native American, Asian/Pacific American and female.

In high school, and since, Janis Ian's "At Seventeen" was my theme song: "I learned the truth at seventeen/That love was meant for beauty queens/ And high school girls with clear-skinned smiles/Who married young and then retired." That song started me thinking about how I dealt with other people, because I am not a relationship person. It takes me a long time to build relationships. I am not one of those people that forms a relationship in the grocery store. Books were my friend. In my teens, it was *Free to Be You and Me*, *Our Bodies, Ourselves*, *Future Shock* and *The Feminine Mystique*.

I initially became an environmentalist because of my mother. She was frugal. She had to be. We wasted nothing. And by wasting nothing, she saved money. We reused everything. We made things out of nothing. You repaired instead of replacing. I realized that this frugality made my mother an environmentalist. When I told her that one day, she told me I was cuckoo. But that's okay, I don't mind. The acorn didn't fall far from that tree. I am also frugal. I have no debt. And I'm planning on keeping it that way.

In eighth grade, I guess someone was upset that a lot of paper was being wasted. So in the lobby of Broughal, they emptied a trophy case and filled it with crumbled paper that was barely used, and certainly it was only used on one side. It was one day's worth. Kaboom. The installation worked. I was all in. I drove people nuts. Then came the creation of Earth Day in 1970.

Fresh out of high school I began working and I started putting everything together. My first paying job was at Kelly Girl Staffing Services for the king's sum of $1.81/hour. Almost everyone was white. We were called Kelly Girls. They still use the name Kelly, but Girls is long gone.

When I got my first job in commercial art at Hess's department store, again the staff was middle-aged, ethnically diverse women and the boss was a man. I worked in the sign shop, in the warehouse near the Fairgrounds. While setting signs letter by letter, I fell in love with typography.

So, I found my art through department store advertising and that introduced me to graphic design. I completed my undergraduate and graduate education through a series of non-traditional programs at Northampton Community College, Cedar Crest College and Marywood University. Now I'm a college instructor and a publisher/art director at Parisian Phoenix. My experiences and beliefs can be seen through my work, some of them probably subconsciously convey the life of a steelworker's daughter.

▶ Gayle F. Hendricks holds an A.A. from Northampton Community College, a B.A. from Cedar Crest College, an MFA from Marywood University and has a decades-long career in graphic design and academia.

The Nail Polish Story

By Angel Ackerman, Eva Parry and Nancy Scott

Child's View

A brilliant idea came to mind when I was getting dressed this morning. I could paint my nails for Nancy! I got my favorite colors and set to work. When my mother got home I was about to apply topcoat. Wow, did they look beautiful!

"I am so stupid!" I exclaimed to my mother as she walked through the door. "I painted my nails for Nancy."

My mother burst out laughing. Nancy couldn't see them anyway. She is blind.

I told Nancy about my nails.

"You know an adult would never have told me that," she observed as she laughed.

Today we went to Dunkin' Donuts. Nancy got a chai and Mommy got an iced coffee. Mommy also bought a dozen donuts. We each ate a donut and I decided to get an iced tea. Mommy let me so I got one and added sugar. I started my Girl Scout homework while Mommy and Nancy worked. Later, I came up with the idea that we should each write a piece on today and compare them. Mommy and Nancy loved it and so here I am writing this now.

Mom's View

I work six days a week in retail. It's not the life I would have chosen for myself, but when it's not crazy like it is right now, it's a lifestyle that allows me the flexibility

to do the other things I deem important, like raise my daughter, travel and work toward my Ph.D. I also harbor delusions of someday recommitting to my writing career — I am a former journalist and my brain dreams in poetry and fiction.

To this end, I work with Nancy, a blind poet and essayist who has been an influence for longer than she knows. I do her typing, send emails and submissions and help find markets. And we also share a healthy competitive spirit that has led to one published poem for me so far.

Today was a Nancy day. We had agreed to meet at 9 a.m., then we would head to Dunkin' Donuts to use their free wi-fi. My almost-twelve-year-old daughter is on spring break and brought a notebook, some homework, and a novel. I decided to splurge and buy a dozen donuts, in part to help amuse the child for a few minutes of the hour-and-a-half Nan and I usually work.

The child is up and down from her seat, but she is trying to be patient. I have made two submissions on Nan's behalf and explain to my daughter how Submittable works. Nan and I find one potential publication a tad immature in its voice, so she sends a piece not quite as polished as her normal work. (Brilliant approach, I tell her.) She asks me if I have certain of her poems she'd like to send to an editor she's neglected. I do. We send them off and Nan tells me to add a note. The phrases Nan reads from her Braille notes reference a blog entry.

"Ah," I say, "the standard reference-to-something-in-that-publication-to-show-that-I-pay-attention line."

She reacts, and I don't remember how, because we start cackling. She and I have both feigned interest in things we don't care about to gain the affection of editors. And we laugh and laugh. Eventually we get a hold of ourselves. We pack up our things and my daughter runs to Nancy's side to pull her toward the car as if they were jockey and race horse. My daughter doesn't quite always recognize the potential hazards in the way... the inevitable 'wet floor sign,' the post, the other people. But somehow, Nancy safely arrives at the car.

Nancy's View

It's nearly five minutes of nine. I open the back door and register bright sun and an idling car.

"Crap," I think. "She beat me."

I'm off to 9 a.m. Dunkin' Donuts with Angel, my computer wizard. The car door opens and I hear running feet. This is not Angel. Then I remember that Eva, Angel's eleven-year-old daughter, is off from school for spring break.

"I forgot about you," I laugh.

"I wanted it to be a good surprise."

Eva's wearing a furry coat. It's exactly what I wanted to wear at (and beyond) her age. I take her well-protected, textured arm.

Eva always guides when she's along. She moves fast.

We manage Dunkin' Donuts' doors but Angel reminds Eva to watch around us because we almost walk into someone I don't hear or find with my cane.

Drinks and doughnuts first. Mine is jelly with granulated (not powdered) sugar. Eva and Angel tell me Eva's Nail Polish Story. I laugh again.

Angel checks web sites and we edit and submit several of my pieces. I am not technological, though I mention the new interesting Braille devices available. Angel is a writer and editor. She knows me well now and helps me do one of the things that keeps me in the world.

Eva tries to write a piece about me, but she doesn't like it. We suggest lists of things she finds intriguing about me or starting with "The Nail Polish Story" and going from there.

The helicopter landing nearby doesn't help. Eva runs out but can't see much. I want to ask her questions, instead of focusing on my Braille task list.

"How do you know the Braille isn't upside down?" Eva wonders.

"Same way you know print is turned, except it feels wrong instead of looks wrong."

"You two are so similar," Eva says. "I love to listen to you work, but I want to work with you, too. What if we all wrote a piece about today?"

"Great idea," we enthuse.

Angel adds, "We could combine them."

"We could submit them," I suggest.

Before I forget too much, I ignore my to do list at home to try a draft. Chai and sugar help. It's fun but too long. I'll edit tomorrow.

▶ Angel R. Ackerman had a 15-year career in print journalism and has dabbled in creative and travel writing. Her Fashion and Fiends novels are available through Parisian Phoenix. Her non-journalism work has been featured in *Dime Store Review*'s 10-word stories, *StepAway Magazine*, *Rum Punch Press*, *Global Studies South*, *Hippocampus Magazine*, The Mighty, Yahoo News and the *SAGE Encyclopedia of Poverty*. Her portfolio and web site is angelackerman.com.

▶ Eva Parry is a high school senior, low brass musician, pet care professional and cat foster and rehab specialist. She hopes to pursue some skill-based education, perhaps auto mechanics in honor of her recently deceased grandfather. She plans to attend either Lafayette College for BS psychology or Moravian University for secondary education.

▶ Nancy Scott's more than 925 essays and poems have appeared in magazines, literary journals, anthologies, newspapers, and as audio commentaries. Her latest chapbook appears on Amazon, *The Almost Abecedarian*. She won First Prize in the 2009 International Onkyo Braille Essay Contest. Recent work appears in *Black Fox Literary Magazine*, *Braille Forum*, *Chrysanthemum*, *Kaleidoscope*, *One Sentence Poems*, *Shark Reef*, *Wordgathering*, and Yahoo News.

The More I Get to Know Me

By Thurston D. Gill Jr.

The more I get to know "Me," the more I realize how messed up I really am.

Much of who I am is a result of a lot of what I did not have control over; how I was raised, genetics, the environment in which I was raised, etc..., no doubt these factors have made a contribution to how messed up I truly am (oh yeah, I forgot to mention all the things I intentionally or unintentionally did to "add the nickel to the dime" of my major malfunctions).

Nonetheless, in prayer, and in times of devotions and meditation, I am reminded of my "super-powers" to be considerate of others, to treat them kindly, gently and justly, and most of all, being patient and extending grace to myself because despite my many flaws, I'm learning to like the guy.

▶ Thurston D. Gill Jr. went from law enforcement to various aspects of the security industry: healthcare & campus security, loss prevention, a private security contractor, and security training & development management. He was ordained as a minister more than 30 years ago and invested several years of life as a mental health recovery specialist and an intensive case manager.

Happy Accident

By Joan Zachary

▶ JOAN ZACHARY moved to Pennsylvania in 1974. She has been intrigued by photography since childhood, but she is also a musician and writer. Currently Joan lives in Point Phillips, Pennsylvania with her fiancé, musician Randall Smith, one very photogenic cat, and the many residents of Plastiqueville.

A Broken Normal

By Eva Parry

For most people, disability and accessibility don't play a role in their day-to-day lives. For others, accessibility plays a major role in every part of their lives. I grew up with two disabled parents, and it never dawned on me that my perception of the world is slightly different than other able-bodied individuals.

Growing up I never considered being raised by two technically disabled parents to be something that effected me as a person. It was like growing up with an alcoholic parent, or a single mom, or any fill-in-the-blank family issue, although outside "the norm," it was just normal to me.

Now that I'm seventeen, I've thought about exactly what parts of my world-view have been influenced by the amount of disability I have been exposed to.

Now that I'm seventeen, I have acquired my own challenges with disabilities. I was born with a slight hearing loss, which I never really thought impacted my life. After recent hearing tests, I found that the loss is not quite as minor as I had previously thought.

This and the change in my perception of the world is a bit different as well as how some people interact with me. It also makes me a bit more critical of others with disabilities and how they go about their life.

As disabilities have become more prominent on social media, it has made me think more about how disabilities have impacted my worldview. In science class when we had to research a science topic for a project, I picked the topic of looking at if plastic straw bans cause accessibility issues. The answer is yes by the way.

I see across social media people who are struggling to live with disabilities because they cannot afford the treatment that keeps them alive and healthy. How many people can't afford the things that keep them alive? More importantly, why is the world's view of disability usually negative? It's seen in comments on videos and posts by disabled people constantly.

"You don't look disabled."

"Why do you need a wheelchair? I've seen you walk in videos."

"You don't need a service dog, you're doing fine."

People with disabilities need to justify a part of them that is impossible to change in order to prove they need accommodations. People who struggle to do simple tasks should not be shamed because their bodies do not work like everyone else's.

My mother has mild Cerebral Palsy, and throughout her life has not learned much about the actual effects that has on her body. She was taught that she had to be just like everyone else even though she struggles to walk and sometimes falls with no visible reason. I learned while still very young to tell her when her legs didn't line up in order to help her adjust. In addition to some of the actual physical problems her CP has caused, it has also caused her to struggle regarding how to ask for help. She struggles asking her employer to accommodate her because she fears that, although she is a good worker, they will look at her differently or even fire her for not being able to keep up with the others.

That may sound stupid. What employer would fire someone who is doing their best with a disability? I suspect a lot of places do. Which adds another struggle for people who need expensive treatments or tools.

If not properly employed, disabled people can't afford the tools to help them live "normally"—but some cannot get jobs in order to pay for said things.

Disabilities also cause insecurities. My father was born with a club hand/ radial arm.[1]

When I was little, I loved it because it was tiny and when I held his hand it fit nicely in mine. But I learned that I wasn't allowed to paint his nails or draw any attention to it, because it was something my father did not like about himself.

There were some things that my dad's clubbed hand/radial arm made harder, or impossible to do, and some days his other hand's arthritis made it so we couldn't play video games together.

I see people with disabilities every day. There are multiple persons with disabilities in my family's circle. My mother's friend, Nancy, is blind.

My neighbor has rheumatoid arthritis. She got diagnosed shortly after she moved in several years ago, in her fifties. She's more financially secure, and therefore is not forced to do things she doesn't want to just to survive. She can call off work if she wants to with little to no consequences.

My mother with her CP, who folds clothes 10 hours a day in the warehouse, almost has panic attacks when she can't go to work because she knows it will effect her paycheck.

The neighbor, on the other hand, has no problem asking her doctor to sign her out of work, and she is prone to skip walking her dog because she hurts too much.

She also spent most of her friendship with my mother complaining about her disability. She complained about not being able to get short-term disability payments and that this might impact her summer vacation rental. My white collar neighbor doesn't appreciate that she has good enough insurance that her doctor can give her a bunch of free medical equipment. Or that her copays and prescription costs are minimal.

I guess what drives me insane is the fact that she doesn't understand that her way of life isn't the common experience for many disabled people. She doesn't appreciate that she gets these luxuries. She also can't admit that she has more power than she thinks to overcome disability. She can't look past her own problems.

Maybe I have a skewed perspective because of what I've seen my parents and plenty of others do.

Most of the people I know with disabilities have had them their entire lives.

---

1 *Editor's Note: See crooked poem, page 18-20*

People with disabilities are just like anyone else. Some of them see life's challenges, make changes, and continue living. Some wallow and let their struggles take them down.

The world should be less cruel to those who have disabilities, yes, but as these adjustments are being made, disabled people should make sure not to give up and continue living as best they can.

▶ Eva Parry is a high school senior, low brass musician, pet care professional and cat foster and rehab specialist. She hopes to pursue some skill-based education, perhaps auto mechanics in honor of her recently deceased grandfather. She plans to attend either Lafayette College for BS psychology or Moravian University for secondary education. She received her first set of hearing aids in January 2022.

How My Life Unfolded—
Some Things Are Meant To Be:
Life in Working Class America

By Maryann Stephanie Ignatz

Now that I am older and looking back, I see it must have been part of a Divine plan. All that happened along the way was preparing me.

I was born on November 3, 1946 on my mother's birthday. She was born in 1914 and my father 1912 so I was an only child to older parents and received the benefit of their values and experiences. Things were tough in 1946, right after World War II, and times didn't boom until the 1950s.

My childhood influences everything in which I have been involved, even today. I have never known a home where people were not coming in and out of the attached tavern— the same is still true now. My dad bought the tavern, Steve's Café on South Main Street in Phillipsburg, N.J., from his father. The tavern has been in our family for more than 100 years. Until I was four or five, it was my extended playroom. It was family-oriented and served working class people from all walks of life.

Behind our home was the Morris Canal towpath, which belonged to the Lehigh Valley Railroad. I played there as a child, finding a lot of coal as, until 1924, the Morris Canal flowed behind the tavern and extended six feet into our present yard. When my great grandpop Steve and grandpop Steve purchased the tavern in 1915, it was called "Morris House." It operated under that name until my dad, Steve III, changed it to Steve's Café in 1939.

My grandpop Steve operated the tavern all throughout Prohibition as a Speakeasy, and I grew up hearing stories of how he had my dad Steve delivering bootleg from false bottom seats in 1929 — when he was 17. That was a promotion from the days when he was six-years-old and cleaning spittoons.

When I was about eight or nine, Dad took Mom and I on rides to show us where the drop points were for the bootleg. All of this plays into what I do today with reunions including bootleggers and offspring from Montana Mountain[1]. They come together to share stories.

In fact, Carl Richline said his grandparents, Emma and John Richline, pulled up by the canal boat and frequented Grandpop Steve's Morris House through the back door.

When I was little, I heard all languages spoken here: Hungarian, Slovak, Italian, Irish brogue, and a lot of broken English. In that broken English, I would hear the old guys say, "You remember my name, I give you nickel." I never forgot so I always got my five cent piece. This exposure led to an

---

1   *Montana Mountain was the local nickname for Warren County's Scott Mountain*

interest in languages from a very young age which influenced me in later life when I became a language teacher.

The barroom always fascinated me. I was four when I started imitating my dad passing out beer in chaser glasses and giving away loose packs of cigarettes from the backbar when he had stepped into the back for something, which gave me the opportunity to be in charge. It was the days of radio and I learned from George Ruft or Jimmy Cagney, "you dirty rat," which I told Dad when he chased me out of the bar for giving stuff away.

He normally was very patient with me as I kept my toys on top of the coke box and he had to move them to get the beer. I stood on the flat top coke box starting as a toddler until I outgrew it.

Music was important and my dad filled the bar when he and his band, "Steve and his Night Owls," entertained on weekends. Dad was a professional musician from 1929 to 1939 retiring when he married. I was four or so, circa 1950, peeking out the door, when they were playing music of the twenties and thirties which I love to this day. Dad played violin, piano, and banjo.

When I turned five, he got me a small violin and taught me to play. Later we could play a great "Sweet Georgia Brown" and "Best Things in Life Are Free" together. He played "Whispering" as a special song for my mom, their song. I know all the old music.

In addition to the canal, the barroom, languages and music, the railroad served as one of the major influences on my life. The Pennsylvania Railroad 18-track switching yard ran along the Delaware River behind our place. The railroaders also frequented the bar. Whether I was in the bar or in the yard, the railroad men made a fuss over me. They gave me silver dollars for my piggy bank.

My dad and I walked the railroad almost every day, as this was one of the ways he relaxed. I was about four when he would sit me on his shoulders and tell me to "hold tight" to his neck while he would grab the ladder side of a box car and we would ride a little ways. He taught me to walk track with baby steps and he taught me to walk ties, too. I loved the smell of creosote. To this day I still carry four pieces of cinder in both knees from a 1950 fall.

My childhood was different in that I was never allowed to walk barefoot because of the tavern. The working men did not carry handkerchiefs and would blow their noses with their fingers, slinging snot over the fence into the yard as well as spitting from chewing tobacco.

We knew all the railroaders — two remained family friends (Walt Gebhard and Les Kober) that helped me gather railroaders in the early 2000s for our once-a-month railroad reunion meetings here at the bar. At that time, we were fighting hard to get the state railroad museum. (I will elaborate more on this later and I will tell the story of how I had the alley behind my home, which is over the actual canal bed, renamed Morris Canal Way.) Morris Canal was dear to my dad when he was growing up. He watched the canal boats go by and went swimming and ice skating on the canal. In fact, my father named the street on Grandpop's tract of land in Alpha "Morris Street" after the Morris Canal, even though the canal didn't go through Alpha.

My father and mother both instilled in me family values, our Hungarian traditions, family history, and the knowledge and love of local history. They loved to share stories of days gone by. Our home was always full of laughter, music and love. My parents, being older, always gave me their time, that was important to them and to me. My father had a great personality and a sense of humor. He taught me to play jokes and have fun. In dealing with people in my later years, this was a special gift.

In early 2000, I had a plaque made that hangs in the bar today. It was a carving of a switching yard engine that I rode on my fourth birthday in 1950— best birthday ever! I got to ride the engine and watch the fireman shovel coal so the Pennsylvania Railroad steam engine could ride me up and down the yard behind our place. Yes, they still had steam engines then.

In the early 1950s, the town sold off the towpath owned by the Lehigh Valley Railroad to property owners. That is when my dad extended our home and tavern over the old towpath. Then he cut a deal with Horlacher Brewery of Allentown. Business boomed. My tavern days were not to be again, until his death when I was 30 in 1977. It got too busy after the expansion as he poured 90-95 full barrels — not halves — per month to a bar three-deep with people and reinforced with rails from the Pennsylvania Railroad. If you go into the cellar, you can see the rails. The section gang put the rails in place during the 1952 remodel.

My childhood was normal, yet different, due to the tavern. When I was four, the Police Commissioner and an officer in uniform came into the bar via the back door to have a drink and also made a fuss over me. I remember sitting on our back porch at age five watching dad's customers riding their horses on the Morris Canal towpath and going into the bar after tying their horses to our back porch.

Today I host events for retired police and firemen. Our neighbors were all Jersey Hose Firemen and their wives belonged to the Auxiliary.

Dad always had old cars. He always took me to the junkyard to get parts for his restoration of a 1929 Model A. He loved cars of the Twenties and Thirties especially, so when I did my Speakeasy event here at the tavern, celebrating our Prohibition history, I was part of Old Town Festival with 1920s and 1930s cars lined up out front. The only one later than that was a 1946 truck, in honor of the year I was born.

Another hobby of Dad's that he shared with me when I was a youngster was to play quoits. It was a good thing he taught me because when I took over the bar in 1977 I had to play. I had two three-timers, which was great for a woman.

Steve's Café is in a working class neighborhood. We grew up picking berries and when dry, I would chew weeds for moisture like my dad taught me. We rode our bikes and watched the trains, everything revolved around the railroad. The chalk for our hopscotch games came from the railroad shanty. Off Center Street there were pens for the animals, like cowboy's pens.

Our lullaby at night was the banging of cars as they made freight for the next day. We even played at the dump. I remember helping the neighbor boy carry a bucket of iron scraps. I helped a neighbor girl pick cigarette butts out of the gutter for her mother to smoke. Her mother even gave us a tin cigar box to put them in.

Until the expansion/remodel of the tavern when I was six, I grew up in

QUOIT FACTORY

www.QuoitFactory.com
5770 Sullivan Trail
Nazareth PA 18064
1-610-762-7335

Official Rules for Slate Quoits and Tailgate Quoits

Pronounced: Quoits is pronounced kwaits

Objective: Player or team to reach 21 points wins the game

Distance: Quoit Boards shall be 18 ft hub to hub

Game Play: 2 or 4 players divided into teams

- Each team is designated 2 rubber quoits

- A coin is flipped to determine who pitches first

- A player's foot may never pass the front of the quoit board when pitching.

- Play alternates between players until all 4 rubber quoits have been pitched. The teamates at the opposing quoit boards tally the score and the winning team begins the next round or until 21 points are reached.

Tips:
- Quoits is a game of strategy and skill. Some players approach the game with the "ringer" mentality and aim for nothing less. Other players enjoy "point" pitching and strategically pitch their quoits snug against the hub making a "dig" extremely difficult.
- "Digging" your opponent's quoit off the board is one of the more exciting game play features to Quoits and is similiar to the game of Shuffleboard.
- Pitching technique is critical and takes practice. Never pitch like horseshoes or across your chest like a frisbee. The quoit will likely bounce off the quoit board. A player must develop a technique similiar to a bowling motion with a release point between their hip and chest. A flat tight spin on the quoit once a player pitches is ideal for aiming and performance.

QUOITS SCORING CHART

RINGER — 3 POINTS		A quoit that lands encircling the hub.
LEANER — 1 POINT		A quoit that lands leaning up against the hub.
DEAD QUOIT — 0 POINTS		A quoit that lands off the game board completely, touches the ground in motion, or lands with any part touching the ground is dead. Remove a Dead quoit from the game board before the next throw. If you do not remove it, any quoit that touches it is also dead.
DAYLIGHT QUOIT		A quoit that lands hanging off the edge of the game board, but not touching the ground. (It's called "Daylight" because you can see light through the hole in the quoit.) Decide before you begin playing if you will allow Daylight quoits, or if you will rule them dead.
CLOSEST QUOIT — 1 POINT		If there are no ringers or leaners, the quoit closest to the hub is worth one point. Use the engraved scoring rings to determine the closest quoit.
RINGER PLUS 1 — 4 POINTS		If you make a ringer and your second quoit lands closer to the hub than either of your opponent's quoits, it is worth one point. Add this to your ringer for a total of 4 points.
TOPPER QUOIT — 3 POINTS		If a ringer is topped by an opponent, the first ringer doesn't score and is cancelled out. The top ringer is worth three points.
TWO TIMER — 6 POINTS		If the same player makes two ringers, one on top of the other, the quoits are worth six points—three points for each quoit.
FOUR TIMER		If all opponents make ringers in their turns, the player with the last ringer wins the game automatically. Achieving a "4 Timer" is extremely difficult and rare.

Used with Permission from the Quoits Factory.

one room upstairs and one room down with an attached shanty with a tin roof and a toilet. This all attached to my dad's barroom.

I wore my cousin's hand-me-downs and when I outgrew them they went to other cousins. We always ate as a family and after supper Dad had a relief bartender there for our rides to Carpentersville. We would go to see the train engine built in Doc Souders yard. Other times we rode to Montana Mountain trying out the dirt roads, where moonshiners sometimes came after us with a shotgun.

After the business boom and the first expansion of the home and tavern in 1952, my parents became prosperous in the 1950s and 1960s. They helped many people, gave to many organizations and donated generously to building the Firth Youth Center, schools, hospitals, and Moravian College Library.

My grandfather Steve died in 1962 and my dad had to use money to renovate 768 South Main. He made the downstairs an old-fashioned barbershop and upstairs became an apartment for his brother, Uncle Dory

Ignatz. The work was completed by 1963. By the fall of 1964, I was ready for college.

I graduated from Phillipsburg High School (with honors) in 1964 and took the college prep course, thanks to a guidance counselor's advice. When I was growing up, we played with dolls and thought of housewife as our future career. Occasionally, I played teacher. Back in the day, girls didn't have much choice.

Bethlehem's Moravian College (now University) became my choice. If you commuted, which I did, it cost $600 a semester, and another $50 for books. It cost $3 for a tank full of gas for Dad's 1961 VW and that took me back and forth to Bethlehem for six days. I belonged to the National Teaching Sorority and graduated at age 21 in spring 1968. I earned a bachelor's degree in Spanish and English and had my certification in Pennsylvania to teach grades seven through 12.

By fall of 1968, I had a job teaching English and Spanish in grades seven through nine in the Easton Area School District. I loved my job, and I got along well with the students. Some of whom come to see me in the tavern and others contact me via Facebook.

My education helped me earn money to help Dad do the final renovation to our home and tavern, making it the place you see today at 766 South Main. The tavern grew with the attached side room. The men no longer had double quoit boards out back. Now they played inside.

My Uncle Dory died in 1966 so we attached the homes and enlarged to a third floor, also adding a sun room and a deck. This was completed by 1975.

After my mom died, I worked at Norton's Liquor Store tutoring my Indian boss. I taught him to read and write in English so my Moravian education came in handy in different ways.

The only way I could cope with the loss was to give up teaching and keep his legacy going, somehow keeping him alive.

I taught until my dad unexpectedly passed away at age 64 on February 2, 1977. He was the third generation of Ignatz to operate the tavern. The tavern was totally for men, and operated by men, with customers whose wives occasionally would accompany them. My father gave me a college education so I would be able to earn my living in a suitable career for a woman.

My father never wanted me in the bar and he had old rules for me; women didn't dye their hair, smoke, nor did they touch a drink. My mother never liked the bar, even though Steve's Café was a clean, respectable working man's bar with good people.

It was my choice to try the bar business — and to be the fourth generation of Ignatz to run Morris House/Steve's Café. My father's death was such a shock. We had just finished the remodel of our home. I had a decision to make. The only way I could cope with the loss was to give up teaching and keep his legacy going, somehow keeping him alive.

My first year in the bar business I learned how to clean the coils for the draft system, how to pitch quoits with the guys, and more importantly, how not to

Commander Robert Radcliffe, my second cousin, CDR, USN, was active duty in the World War II, Korean and Vietnam wars. His wife, Irma Senkovits Radcliffe, was an artist in San Diego and a gallery owner. Some of her work—tigers—hangs in the back bar. Both received burial at Arlington National Cemetery in Washington, D.C.

When Commander Radcliffe visited the bar, it was his first exposure to Quoits and he enjoyed watching the game.

Other family included my second cousin Ethel Senkovits, of Huntington Beach, Calif., was a nuclear physicist. She worked at NASA during the moon landing and contributed to the design of space suits. She left me a model of the interior of a spacecraft, her Boeing awards, her government awards, and some jewelry.

Robert Jenney, a Jazz trombonist, married my cousin Joan. He performed in a variety of bands, including greats like Tommy Dorsey and Fred Waring Orchestra.

Grandpop Steve's brother Paul Ignatz changed his name to Joseph Evans when he left Reno, Nevada, and landed in Los Angeles where he owned a nightclub and lived in the Hotel Biltmore with his wife, Linda, a lumber heiress. Paul/Joseph was a friend of Groucho Marx. The two often went shopping together. Yes, Groucho Marx did his own shopping. Paul/Joseph and Linda also visited the tavern. Both remained generous to the Ignatz family.

be shy and reserved as I had been. I even learned to laugh at myself. We had loyal customers and I operated the tavern with Dad's rules and Dad's prices.

We sold a seven-ounce beer and two shots of bar whiskey for $1. All the men — good people — had to get used to a woman behind the bar. The guys helped me, respected me and told me to wear a baggy shirt and baggy pants, there was no more reason to be dressing like a teacher. It was the best decision I could have made. Now, I was continuously learning from people who were older than myself from many walks of life with their many experiences.

I was 30, and except for two others, the customers ranged in age from 48 to 96 sharing their personal stories and local history. We had teachers, steel workers, union heads, working men from all the area factories, junk pickers, postal workers, railroaders, insurance salesmen, janitors, factory owners, construction workers, police officers (including the chief), professors, mechanics, etc. Most of the men were veterans— either of World War II or the Korean War. Many veteran-themed events grew out of this, even today, adding Vietnam classmates and war hero Joe Belardo, filling our bar to capacity. Belardo, from Plainfield, who wrote the book *Dusterman Vietnam: Story of the Last Great Gunfighters*, hosted a program at the tavern for the 50th anniversary of his service, April 22, 2017. He was highly decorated with three purple hearts, a bronze star with valor, and numerous Marine and Army citations.

The tavern business was good, and it seemed like I was meant to be there.

It never felt like work to me, but a social group of great people. I had Sundays off and Mom and I went on rides and spent time with her family. It was good that I was home with her in the bar, because she missed my dad very much.

In 1986, the town of Phillipsburg sold off three dilapidated buildings next to our home, tavern and barbershop. I joined this venture of cleaning up the neighborhood by buying the buildings and knocking them down, as they were a fire hazard. I extended our yard, making it a showplace with beautiful plants. My mom taught me about flowers and plants and we even had a small garden. I considered it an investment in case I got married, then I could extend the building, have space for a commercial kitchen if I needed it, and still have room for a parking area. This, despite my plan, was not meant to be.

When Dad died, we also had to oversee the management of the barbershop which included a license in the name of "Steve's Barbershop." My education came in handy with all the business paperwork. I dealt with the lawyer but Dad's passing left me to do a lot of the work myself. I filled out the licenses for the tavern and the barbershop and I did the taxes.

In 1997, when Mom was 83, she became ill. I now became a caregiver. She had always spoiled me by doing everything for me: cooking, laundry, cleaning. Now I had to do the best I could while tending bar and supervising Steve's Barbershop. We had a hospital bed in the living room for Mom, and God was with me as I became not only a caregiver, but a good caregiver thanks to my mom's instruction. She stayed mentally sharp until her death on Christmas Eve, December 24, 2005.

Other notables who visited the tavern:

Rachael Ferrara, set designer in Los Angeles nominated for an Emmy

Jim Hontz, general manager at Nazareth Speedway. The speedway traces its roots to 1910 where it began life as a horse racing track. The original track was demolished in 1988 and developed into a shopping center. The large track opened in 1966 but has an on-again, off-again history best known for launching the careers of the drivers in the Andretti family.

Jack Kromer, auto racing photographer who spent almost 50 years in the business. He got his start thanks to Jim Hontz giving him press credentials at Nazareth Speedway.

Robert Stem, neighborhood boy who played for Syracuse and pro-football in the AFL for the Boston Patriots

Christine Wilson, Phillipsburg native and season ten Hell's Kitchen winner, who became a head chef at Gordon Ramsay Steak in Paris Las Vegas. She went on to supervise multiple restaurants in the North American branch of Ramsay's culinary empire.

In fact it was Mom that encouraged me to pursue media coverage in print and on television in order to help preserve our history and to fight for Phillipsburg to earn the designation as future site of the official New Jersey transportation museum[2].

The tavern has its own history. In the 1970s, when my dad was here, Ken Kercheval (actor most well-known for his role as Cliff Barnes on Dallas) would stop by and, for fun, tended bar here a few times. He shared my dad's interest in Packards.

In the 1980s, Doug DeLuca, then a producer on Jimmy Kimmel Live, used to drink here. He even wrote a great letter that I display in the bar, beside the one from Mike Zinski of London, England, Cincusnaveur, Naval Forces Europe, who used Eisenhower's World War II office. We also met Ross

2 Editor's note: The official name of the transportation museum is the New Jersey Transportation Heritage Center. The project has been under development for more than 25 years and information can be found at friendsnjthc.org

Edward Percifield, a poet, who wrote the poem, "Our History in Rhyme," dedicated to Steve's Café.

Because of Mom's idea to preserve this rich heritage, I maintained an emphasis on local history from 2000 forward. At age 88, in 2002, Mom had a stroke and could still be found on the hospital bed in the living room. I cut back the tavern hours so I had more time to sit with her, and I sat with her at all hours. That gave me more time to collect and curate historical photos to display in the tavern. And we still had the barbershop to oversee.

To help finance Mom's care, I sold a ring that Uncle Joe, remember Uncle Joe who had changed his name and moved to California, had left us. It was a beautiful ring with three high quality diamonds, each more than a carat. I sold it to a jeweler for only a third of what it was worth. Later, I saw the ring again when I was working at Norton Cork and Bottle. A woman was wearing it and I confirmed it was the same ring because my uncle's name was engraved in it. The ring was valued at $30,000. I sold it for $9,000 to the jeweler and this woman paid $20,000.

The woman said to me she never visited Norton's on South Main Street, but that day she knew she couldn't pass by.

Also while Mom was ill, this was the same time we asked the town to rename the alley behind our home to Morris Canal Way, as it was, as mentioned before, directly over the canal bed. We turned down the honor of naming the street Ignatz Lane, as offered by Mayor Harry Wyant, in the interest of the broader history. The town needed a proper name on the alley to enable proper maintenance on the road.

At this time I met more people and historians, including Captain Bill McKelvy[3] of the Friends of the New Jersey Transportation Heritage Center.

As a result of all the discussion in town, Bill stopped by to see me and later published my historic walking tour of the block surrounding the tavern in the transportation museum newsletter. I had compiled the walking tour based on information my father told me and supplemented that with details from my older neighbors (such as Alex Pruznick) and even customers.

Through Captain Bill's newsletter, I met Myra Snook of the Warren County Canal Committee. (She was also a fan of Ken Kercheval.) With Myra's help, we had the historic marker placed in the alley stating that "the Morris Canal crossed here." She photographed the block as I pointed out areas of interest. Through this project, I met Bob Barth, then president of the New Jersey Canal Society. There was a big interest in the tavern and surrounding property, as I mentioned earlier, this was the former Morris House, where canal men could get off their boats and come in the back door in the days when Grandpop first bought this place in 1915.

I worked with many historians: Jim Lee, Sr., a conductor for Jersey Central, a customer and the author of canal books; Jim Lee, Jr., his son; old-time customer Carl Baxter and Ron Wynkoop, the founders of the Phillipsburg Historical Society; and Wayne Sherrer, a neighbor and president of the society. I conducted interviews with many of my neighbors, recording memories of the canal such as those from Frank Vargo on Lock Street. Many were published by Captain Bill and computerized by Jim Lee.

3 Editor's note: Learn more about Bill at https://www.lhry.org/mckelvey

I also wrote the interviews I conducted with the railroaders and one especially interesting one was with Walt Gebhard when he was in his nineties.

Captain Bill continued the fight to bring the state railroad museum to Phillipsburg, which gave me the idea to form the "Rusty Spikes." The Rusty Spikes became a club of about 25 retired railroaders—in their 70s, 80s and 90s. The group met monthly at the tavern and my friend Ron Luckock ran a "beer train" on the bar which delivered drinks while the men watched a railroad slide show. Jim Pruznick videotaped interviews with the men. Paul Carpenito, president of the Phillipsburg Railroad Historians, would stop in as well. Captain Bill was often there.

Myself and the railroaders of my childhood—we all appeared on television (four times!) and the tavern was featured in multiple newspapers: *Star-Ledger, Phillipsburg Chronicle, Free Press, Warren Reporter,* and the *Express-Times* among them. We also reached a few magazines and historical journals.

We would often have entertainment, mainly musicians but occasionally a medicine man show which brought Mom back to her childhood when the medicine men would do shows from the train in Brainards. It seemed fitting to have all these railroad connections since in the early days of his business, my dad had sponsored a "Rail Busters" ball team.

Here we are, early 2000s, reaching the press and working toward a transportation museum in Phillipsburg. I started creating promotional souvenirs for our historic bar, such as mugs, teddy bears and a beanie baby mule, all of which highlighted the historic and multi-generational legacy of the bar. I donated some of these items to the railroad museums and to the canal museum at Waterloo Village. My goal was to preserve history and help bigger causes, such as the transportation center.

My favorite television coverage appeared on local channel two, which devoted a lot of time not only to the tavern but also to the barbershop, which we kept as an old style shop out of the 1930s. Ron Luckock appeared with me, running his beer train. The train, as it appeared in the video, ran down the bar delivering a beautiful beer that kept its creamy head.

Even my mother gave me a compliment on the coverage, and mothers of my generation did not give out compliments in fear that their children would get a big head. She said to me, "That woman is intelligent. She knows what she is talking about. She is beautiful. That's not you."

She said these things in April 2005 and she passed away in December. Mom's wish was that I close the bar and sell the license, because she didn't want someone else operating a bar here with the "Steve" name.

My education served me well in performing the business administration tasks of the tavern and it also helped me with this historic preservation push. People I encountered also had a hand in that. God sent those people throughout my life when I needed them.

When Mom died, Myra Snook gave me some money toward my efforts to keep Morris House/canal history alive in the tavern. Bill Ziviski was also a help, and sadly I found his body in February 2006. I found him in the senior housing building where he lived, two months to the day of Mom's passing. His daughter called me to check on him, and of course I did as he was a family friend and loyal customer.

So now life had changed again. It was the first time I was ever alone here. One year I operated the bar seven days a week, and there were still not enough people to keep me from getting lonely. My cousin Margaret and my cousin Barbara (Bubby) were there for me. We would go out to eat. Bubby and I went through Dad's coin collection as I needed to sell some of it. I no longer had Mom's social security as a financial help. Margaret took me to Saint Phillip and Saint James Catholic Church where I was a member and became more active.

It was my beer driver, Randy Wilson, who said I wasn't the same and he suggested I get a part-time job at Norton's Liquor Store also on South Main Street. So that's what happened. I worked part-time and ran the bar part-time as I tried to sell the license, as my mom had suggested. I continued to celebrate railroad day at the bar. And on railroad day in May 2006, something happened.

My second cousin on my mother's side, Helen "Holly" Witlin looked me up after she found the family history I wrote when her mom died. Carl Baxter brought her to meet me. She was from Norristown, Pa., and we became close like sisters. God put her in my life and in January 2009, her husband John bought my double lot— that double lot I had made my showplace of flowers and plants and held in preparation of my potential future. John bought it for $50,000 which saved me from credit cards. They then donated the lot to Habitat for Humanity. Holly visited often and provided moral support.

Steve could make you forget your problems even on your worst day.

I loved the people I met and served at Norton's. I loved the job and it was hard to believe the only other job I had had outside the tavern was as a teacher 30 years prior. This allowed me to test my personality.

There many people knew my dad and they talked well of him. What a wonderful legacy he had left! The consensus was that Steve could make you forget your problems even on your worst day.

Everyone agreed that my dad had a great sense of humor and personality. People brought me gifts when I worked at Norton's and told me I made them feel good even on a bad day. Three times I almost sold the license, but every time something made the deal fall through. I thought I would sell the lots, then the liquor license and continue working at Norton's. But in Spring 2013, I developed bad sinus problems due to allergies and returned to the bar full-time. It seemed like the hand of destiny again!

Steve's Barbershop closed as my barber finally bought his own place. And honestly, the rules to run a barbershop in the state of New Jersey had changed and it had gotten to be too much to keep that license. To make my life easier, I sought town permission to operate the building as an office, and with the town's blessing, I rented it in 2012 to a taxi operator. That's what still occupies that office today.

There was not much business left as most of the regulars had passed away. I had spent too many hours at the liquor store to build new clientele. My classmate Anthony "Pip" Piperata brought his friend (author and motivational speaker) Billy Staples to see me. The idea was for me to reinvent, find my niche and get some publicity.

Steve's Café, the historic Morris House, turned 100 years old on May 25, 2015. The Chamber of Commerce awarded me the milestone award at their annual banquet. There I announced that I wanted to give back to the community by allowing organizations to meet at Steve's Café for free but with a cash bar.

Billy appointed me the chairwoman of the first Phillipsburg Author's Book Day for the BEST Scholarship Foundation, which also gave me press. I started giving talks for local groups including the Phillipsburg Downtown Association.

Other family members:

Eric Rosa, vice president of Beverly Hills Bank

Anna Deri Schopfné, officer at the Budapest Bank in Hungary

Major Andy Sipos

Lt. JG Margaret Sipos

Richard & Laura Sipos, pilot a 1960 open cockpit, dual control airplane

Dr. Sándor Sipos, delivered the Prime Minister of Hungary's baby

Marshall Stacker, recently ran in the Miata sports class at Indianapolis Speedway.

The book event also strengthened my relationship with local daily newspaper, *The Express-Times*. Editor Jim Deegan spoke with me about that event and I mentioned my recognition from the Chamber of Commerce. He did a lovely story that ended up on the front page and even sent photographer Sue Beyer.[4] A lot of publicity was falling into place.

Now in the 100th anniversary story, I mentioned Grandpop's Speakeasy. This brought Richard Dalyrymple Jr. to see me as he was doing a book, *The Bootleggers of Montana Mountain*. He devoted a chapter and some photos to the café and my father. In 2017, we celebrated as part of Old Town Festival with the car show, costumes, period music and of course, sales of the book. We even sold four dozen special edition Ignatz-Morris Speakeasy t-shirts. I signed about 96 autographs on that day alone. And other children of the Montana Mountain bootleggers attended the event.

Plus, I got to reconnect with old friends. David Hadju, a professor at Columbia University who was nominated by President Biden for the National Countil on the Humanities, always played quoits at Steve's Café with his father and his brother whenever he came to town. He came to the book event upon my invitation.

I would like to add that several mayoral administrations supported my events—Mayors Wyant, Ellis and Tersigni—even attending my 40 years in business party in 2017. *Lehigh Valley Business Journal* featured the tavern, "How to Keep 100-year-old Business Going." My family business even made it to the members of the Lehigh Valley Chamber of Commerce. I hope all of this would make my dad proud of his shot-and-beer tavern. I know his little girl is. (Me.) I grew up thinking everything was a saloon just like the westerns on TV I even called the beauty salon a saloon.

4 Editor's note: That story can be read here, https://tinyurl.com/4d2m8chy

Today, I am happy to say we do many community events in addition to regular, monthly railroad meetings. And of course, we have the firemen, veterans, and Hibernians. Other groups, like the retired police or reunion classes, hold yearly events. In 2019, we started our racing event, where I know five generations of the family.

I like the way James Long summed it up, "No amount of money could buy the rich legacy you have here. Your dad was special: walking the rails with you, riding box cars, taking you to junk yards, letting you drive the Packard when you were only 13. No one else has memories like that. He made you a fun person. He gave you what no money can buy."

All I can say is that it was meant to be.

▶ Maryann Stephanie Ignatz graduated Phillipsburg High School and Moravian College. She taught Spanish and English in the Easton Area School District for almost a decade before her father's death in February 1977. Since then, she has been the proprietor of Steve's Cafe, a shot-and-beer, working man's tavern at 766 South Main Street in Phillipsburg, N.J.

Neurodivergence as Resistance

By Jessica R. Dreistadt, Ph.D.

Normativity oppresses;
Dogma suppresses.
Their expectations and their borders and their rules
provoke separation, exceptionalism, and dominance.
Connection threatens their existence.

Connection of people decenters normativity,
Connection of ideas questions dogma.
Through connection, all is possible.
Ideas are uncontained and unrestrained,
Patterns emerge,
Brilliant colors swirl,
Hearts are healed,
People are free.

Think differently. Feel more. Be fluid. Get labeled.
Such pain invites creativity:
A search for reconciliation and meaning,
A desire for purpose and understanding.
Such longing creates
while normativity and dogma takes.

▶ Jessica R. Dreistadt, Ph.D., is the founding director of The Fruition Coalition and the author of 11 books about leadership and social change. Her recently completed dissertation, "Portraits of Women Leaders: Solidarity and Social Division in Progressive Social Movement Organizations," explored the complex ways that identities constrain and facilitate relationships. To connect with Jessica, visit www.jessicardreistadt.com

Woke

By Dawn Heinbach

Don't tell me how progressive you are
when you cannot even acknowledge
another person's oppression, whitesplaining that
they are somehow to blame for their situation.

Don't tell me how cool you are
when at Halloween you throw a colorful sash over your shoulder and
on your head is a huge sombrero ringed with pom poms.
In one hand, you carry a bottle of Tequila.
You slur your words when you explain that you're the drunk Mexican.

Don't tell me that you're an advocate for social change
when you get frustrated that people are blocking traffic
trying to manifest that change.
"Doesn't anyone work anymore?" you mutter as you lay on the horn.

Don't tell me that you're an ally
when the next black person is killed by a policeman using excessive force
and you post on social media:
"All Lives Matter"
and
"They should have listened to the police."

Don't tell me that you're [codeswitch] down with the sisterhood
when you don't know
who Tamir Rice is
and why he is dead.

Don't congratulate yourself
for being on the "right" side
because you didn't vote for Trump
when you didn't vote for Hillary either,
because, you know, her emails.

Don't tell me that
it's hard to be white
until you've been mistaken
for a terrorist
because of your beard —

until you've been passed up for a promotion
for the fourth time
and watch as it is given to a white lesser qualified employee
who was hired six years after you —
until you notice a group of white people move
to the opposite side of the street
to avoid passing near you
and your brown-skinned friends
on the sidewalk.

Don't tell me you're a feminist
when you witness another women's tearful reaction
to dehumanizing words
and describe it as "having a meltdown."
"She should toughen up" is your advice.

Don't tell me how progressive you are
when Black football players kneel to protest
police brutality
and you say,
"They should go back where they came from."

Until you have been the only white person
in a room,
on a bus,
at work,
at school —
and have been conscious of your skin's lack of pigment,
like a polar bear in a midnight sea —
don't tell me how you "don't see color."

Don't tell me how woke you are.

Don't tell me.

Don't.

▶ Dawn Heinbach holds an M.A. in Publishing from Rosemont College and is completing a master's degree in journalism at New York University. In 2016, her poem "Stunning" earned an award from the English department at Kutztown University of Pennsylvania. In 2015, Heinbach founded Writing Wrongs, a 501(c) (3) nonprofit that facilitates a literary journalism program for college students. She lives in Berks County with her partner of 25 years and their two rescue cats..

An "Ear"ie Interview

By Angel Ackerman with Eva Parry

Eva Parry has always loved music— from the iPod shuffle that played in her nursery to the four years she spent in marching band. She can't walk by a brass instrument without trying to play it. From a very young age, she could distinguish between languages even though she couldn't speak them.

But Eva has also always had ear issues, chronic ear infections that corresponded with the change of seasons and fluid constantly in her head. She never caught colds, only ear infections and the occasional strep throat.

She had her first set of ear tubes in first grade. She came home after her first day back to school and cried. Her teacher yelled at them all day, she said, and the cafeteria was so loud she had to put her head down on the table and cover her ears.

She had her second set of ear tubes in November 2019—when she was fifteen. This time the doctor removed her adenoids. This distressed Eva, because, to her surprise, her nose suddenly worked. Until then, she had never experienced a runny nose. Until then, she never experienced inhaling cold air into her nostrils and ending up with the same cold air in her throat.

Now, Eva is seventeen and she changed from her pediatrician who insisted she never had any ear problems to a family practice, so she changed ENT practices, too. That revealed some truths about her hearing that she knew but had never confirmed.

ANGEL: Tell me about your ears.
EVA: They don't work. They are just enough of an issue to be an inconvenience.

ANGEL: But they do work, you are very gifted musically.
EVA: Music is loud.

ANGEL: Is that why you play brass?
EVA: It's a lot easier to hear lower things.

ANGEL: What about high-pitched things?
EVA: They get lost

ANGEL: Is it congenital?
EVA: Some of it, yes. Probably most of it. My dad is completely deaf in one ear and my mom can't hear the highest tones on the spectrum.

ANGEL: What can you tell me about your series of hearing tests?
EVA: My first ENT was super predictable, in part because I had gone for

a decade, my brain would predict when I should hear the next tone. My brain really thought I heard them. When I went to a new ENT, the test was sporadic and I couldn't tell if it was a legitimate sound.

The results were more extreme, because I couldn't tell I was missing something.

The doctor said that one tube had fallen out, and removed the other. The ENT said we would wait to see how I would do in the coming months, but the audiologist suggested I was a candidate for hearing aids.

Being able to hear better would be cool, but I'm not 1,000 percent sure that I need hearing aids.

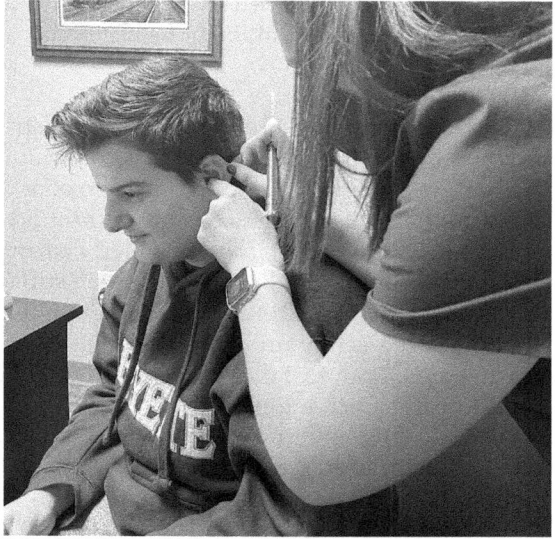

ANGEL: That's your only reservation.
EVA: I'm concerned about the cost, because if I need them for the rest of my life, I'm going to have to pay for them and they are expensive. I never know if it's just me or if no one can hear those things or if my teacher is just being quiet today.

ANGEL: How does the prospect of hearing aids feel?
EVA: Exciting but nerve-wracking. I should be able to hear my teachers and all the things I should hear but the things I already hear will be louder and that might be uncomfortable. I'm also wondering if I'm going to have to change out my hearing aids and my headphones.

I don't think people at school, except for a handful of teachers, know I have a hearing problem.

If I go to school one day randomly with hearing aids, are people going to think they are hallucinating? Did I always have them? Or will they say, "those are new." I guess I'm interested in people's reactions.

I didn't realize I had that much of a hearing problem until I became a waitress. My parents and teachers have clear speaking voices. I didn't realize how many people don't.

I didn't realize how much I relied on lip reading. I knew I did it, but I always thought it was a fall-back "just in case." Then, Covid happened and everyone was wearing masks. Those who did speak clearly, now I struggled with them. Those who didn't, I didn't have a clue what they were saying.

I felt really bad because when I worked in the restaurant, a lot of people around me were Hispanic and had thick Spanish accents. I couldn't understand them, but it wasn't because of their accent. I felt bad because people must misunderstand them all the time.

So, do you have a disability?

I don't think so. I'm not sure. Technically, being hard of hearing is a disability but it doesn't seem to put me at such an extreme disadvantage that I would consider myself disabled. I don't need anything special to live my life. It would be nice. But it's not a necessity.

UPDATE FROM EVA:

Throughout my life, I had noticed that I struggle to hear people in crowds or when they speak quietly and was continuously reminded by my family that my speaking voice is loud. I had no concept that my experience was different than the experience of others around me.

Recently, I got Signia in-ear, molded hearing aids. At first, I didn't notice much of a change, and I sometimes even still (after two weeks), doubt that they make much of a difference in other people's speaking voices. The main thing I noticed is that my voice has volume now. When I'm not wearing my hearing aids, I can feel the difference in volume in my vocal cords, but the voice I hear is unchanging.

After dealing with the plethora of technical issues associated with getting a new piece of technology to assist in your daily life, I think that they have definitely improved my hearing in a helpful way.

This begs the question; am I disabled? I've pondered this question for quite a while now. I guess in a practical sense I am, but I've always thought that I am not disabled enough.

▶ Angel R. Ackerman had a 15-year career in print journalism and has dabbled in creative and travel writing. Her Fashion and Fiends novels are available through Parisian Phoenix. Her non-journalism work has been featured in *Dime Store Review*'s 10-word stories, *StepAway Magazine*, *Rum Punch Press*, *Global Studies South*, *Hippocampus Magazine*, The Mighty, Yahoo News and the *SAGE Encyclopedia of Poverty*. Her portfolio and web site is angelackerman.com.

▶ Eva Parry is a high school senior, low brass musician, pet care professional and cat foster and rehab specialist. She hopes to pursue some skill-based education, perhaps auto mechanics in honor of her recently deceased grandfather. She plans to attend either Lafayette College for BS psychology or Moravian University for secondary education.

Standing

By Nancy Scott

On this Veterans' Day, I wear the thin jacket. Most years, I'm tucked in hooded fleece with gloves. Veterans' Day is often the first time I wear gloves in any winter but I'm not going very far this time. Just far enough to honor a tradition.

I arrive a few minutes early and strain my ears. I almost hear the parade a few blocks away. I applaud the probable flag-bearers and the 21-gun salute, which is the only thing I can hear, in case the dead relatives are watching. I want them to know I am still loyal and grateful. But, Anne can't drive anymore so I'm alone at the edge of my building's upper parking lot.

The year before, Anne and I stayed near our parking lot close to her car. Because I can't see, Anne's narration helped me watch the elementary school children come outside with their construction paper flags. Anne was no longer strong enough to walk any of the four-block parade route. Certain grades came out of certain doors. Anne said there was a teacher in front and a teacher behind each section. I didn't know last year would be Anne's last Veterans' Day parade. No more following the one high school band to the four veterans' memorials. No more covering my ears at each stop. No more comforting restaurant hot pepper pot soup afterwards.

Drums from two blocks away beat time that's present and past. They herald how we all try. Two young trumpeters echo "Taps" and "Amazing Grace." Every year, the band plays the same medley of songs from each service branch. This probably allows for less practice time.

Local veterans' organizations are vanishing— no marching, fewer monthly gatherings of old widows. Those of us left stand for standing; a proof and a prayer

not just for those who've died. Is it the absence of tradition that makes us old?

The fourth and last corner is closest to my audio vantage. I know what's happening because of multiple years taking part in this event. Most of the speeches are done at the first stop. By my fourth corner, everyone is ready for the calls and the guns.

Wind tries to pull me off balance. I lean on my cane, wishing for something to hold onto. I think that winter is trying to appear. I cover my ears with chilled hands.

But afterwards, I hear more people than usual applauding. I hope many of them are young. I hope they embrace changes that are coming and the echoes of the past that accompany them.

The trumpeters' last playing of "Taps" and "Amazing Grace" is beautiful in the crisp autumn air.

And then, many feet move toward home and school and errands. The band marches away. The police allow traffic to resume. The receding drums echo off buildings. I stand still until I can't hear any feet or drums.

▶ Nancy Scott's more than 925 essays and poems have appeared in magazines, literary journals, anthologies, newspapers, and as audio commentaries. She has a chapbook, *The Almost Abecedarian* (on Amazon), and won First Prize in the 2009 International Onkyo Braille Essay Contest. Recent work appears in Braille Forum, *Disabilities Studies Quarterly*, *Philadelphia Stories*, *Pentimento* and *Wordgathering*.

Wishing I Could Say No

LESSONS FROM LIFE AS THE YOUNGEST

By Jan Krieger

Being the youngest child on both sides of my extended family made it terribly difficult for me to impress anyone with my accomplishments. Anything spectacular I attained elicited the same reaction: "Well, we expected that!"

Yup, never matter the achievement — forming sentences at nine months old, honor society in high school, early decision to the college of my choice, perfect pitch at age six (like I had ANY control over that...) — it was expected.

As a result, I determined my role in this hierarchy to be that of the jokester and entertainer, the peacemaker, the "yes" gal, ensuring everyone was happy and everything was smooth.

The one time I did stretch my wings in a fit of independence, I moved to a suburb of DC, chasing that ever elusive engagement ring.

How cosmopolitan, I thought - the parties, the shows, the restaurants, the shopping, everything a major city could offer!! Instead it was more like work, the gym, dinner at Roy Rogers, and 28-mile traffic jams.

In addition to that excitement, NO bling!!! So after almost five years of that action, I packed and returned to home base.

The timing was very apropos, as I was able to help my family care for our beloved dad who passed several months thereafter. It seemed like in quick succession I was losing everyone near and dear, especially my mom and sister who died 18 days apart.

Although most of my relatives have moved on to the great beyond, I am here and still saying yes. Make a donation? Sure, how much you need? Run for school board? Happy to do that. Pet sit for how long? Of course! I think you get my drift.

Not too long ago, my good friend and neighbor, herself a prolific and published journalist, approached an eclectic group of her interesting associates, myself included, with an idea to create an anthology of unique, personal essays written by this savvy crowd.

As usual my response was "OK."

Ugh, "OK."

How could she not see that in this case "OK" was really code for "No?" Nope. *Nyet.* Heck to the no. I think not.

Therein lies the rub!

I'm very much a wordy stickler for spelling and grammar. But how I do like the written word? Reading it — LOVE LOVE LOVE.

But writing it????

Composing my master's thesis, mandatory to earning the degree, almost did me in. Somehow I managed to squeeze out twenty-seven pages, with part of it in Russian transliteration. See I told you about being spectacular: *Shto vi khotitye znyat po-russki?!!!*

Anyway, I'd been laying low since that initial contact. Had lots of other tings to do — meetings, shopping for a multitude of birthdays, learning a new baton routine for the alumni band Homecoming performance (I didn't drop either) — important stuff.

Then last night came the follow up email, advising the pieces due by end of week. Oopsie!!

Time to own up that I had nothing to contribute so far. With curiosity getting the best of me, I wondered how long some of the already completed submissions ran. I was not ready to hear from one to twenty pages!!!

After regaining consciousness, I realized it was time to girl up and do this.

The architect of this anthology was kind enough to offer several ideas for me to explore. Let's examine them:

- Experiencing the early years of co-education at Lafayette College: or as I call it, 1500 men to 500 women and still no date for the big game weekend.

- Studying Russian during the Cold War: or, no way my parents were letting me go to the Soviet Union over winter break.

- Being the Jewish lady who bakes a multitude of Christmas cookies: or, I need to get a Kitchen-Aid mixer,

- Losing your family while young and people forget your loneliness: or, time marches on, you heal, but it still leaves a gaping hole in your heart.

Seems like my attempt to write an essay is more like a *Seinfeld* episode — a lot about nothing, Yet still entertaining. Maybe this little blurb will be included in the upcoming anthology, maybe not.

Just trying to do my part, Making sure all is copacetic, everyone is satisfied. Some things never change.

But really — didn't you expect that of me???

PS—Just when I thought we were done, the editor texted and asked for revisions. And, as usual, I said yes.

▶JAN KRIEGER is not a best selling novelist. After a 30-plus-year career in the travel industry, she is now happily learning the craft of being a chocolatier. She graduated from Wilson Area High School, holds a B.A. in Russian from Lafayette College, an M.A. in Slavic Languages and Literatures from Pennsylvania State University, and a certificate of travel and tourism from Northampton Community College — in that order.

Thoughts About Everyday Life

By Thurston D. Gill Jr.

Distance Learning
I've been on this earth long enough to know that chaos is best observed from a distance.

I Sometimes Go Too Far
I've concluded that there are some things I am just not supposed to figure out.

Instead of waiting to receive some insight into a matter, I plod around in the dark, going beyond any light or revelation, then I just fill in any gaps of what I don't know with my brand of ignorance.

Stinkin Thinkin
When I believe too much of the wrong things and have little trust in the right things.

My Listening
When I am "listening" to others in conversation, it often helps me to clarify and express my thoughts and feelings. Sometimes, I must initiate or feed the conversation, but essentially, I MUST LISTEN!

A lot of times, I won't even know what to say until I listen to what is said.

People Pleasin'
As a Christian man, I am called upon daily to please someone, at some cost to myself, but never everyone, at all cost.

▶ Thurston D. Gill Jr. went from law enforcement to various aspects of the security industry: healthcare & campus security, loss prevention, a private security contractor, and security training & development management. He was ordained as a minister more than 30 years ago and invested several years of life as a mental health recovery specialist and an intensive case manager.

Spasticity: Walking with Cerebral Palsy

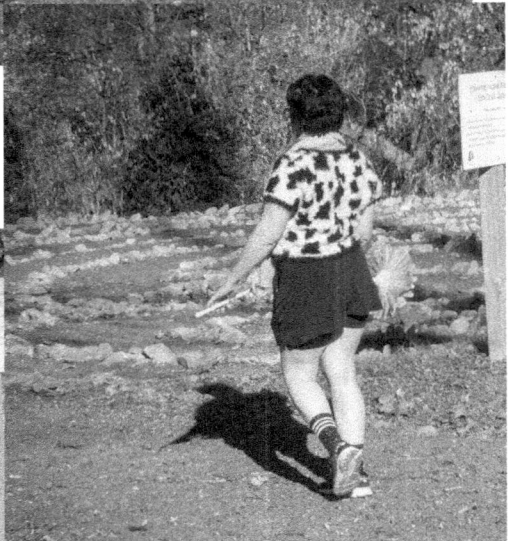

Photos by Joan Zachary

*Photos taken on the
Karl Stiner Arts Trail, Easton, Pa.*

Index

www.ingramcontent.com/pod-product-compliance
Lightning Source LLC
Chambersburg PA
CBHW071115030426
42336CB00013BA/2088